T0384364

The Supply Chain: A System in Crisis

The Supply Chain: A System in Crisis

Edited by

Stefan Gold

Professor of Sustainability Management, Faculty of Economics and Management, University of Kassel, Germany

Andreas Wieland

Associate Professor of Supply Chain Management, Department of Operations Management, Copenhagen Business School, Denmark

Cheltenham, UK • Northampton, MA, USA

Published by
Edward Elgar Publishing Limited
The Lypiatts
15 Lansdown Road
Cheltenham
Glos GL50 2JA
UK

Edward Elgar Publishing, Inc.
William Pratt House
9 Dewey Court
Northampton
Massachusetts 01060
USA

A catalogue record for this book
is available from the British Library

Library of Congress Control Number: 2024930583

This book is available electronically in the **Elgar**online
Business subject collection
http://dx.doi.org/10.4337/9781803924922

ISBN 978 1 80392 491 5 (cased)
ISBN 978 1 80392 492 2 (eBook)

Printed and bound by CPI Group (UK) Ltd, Croydon, CR0 4YY

Contents

PART III   WAYS OUT OF THE CRISIS

Contributors

Philip Beske-Janssen, Department of Operations Management, Copenhagen Business School, Denmark

Vikram Bhakoo, University of Melbourne, Australia

Sandra L. Fisher, Münster School of Business, FH Münster, Germany

Stefan Gold, Faculty of Economics and Management, University of Kassel, Germany

Graham Heaslip, HUMLOG Institute, Hanken School of Economics, Helsinki, Finland; Atlantic Technological University, Galway, Ireland

Pasi Heikkurinen, LUT Business School, Finland; Department of Economics and Management, University of Helsinki, Finland

Johanna Hohenthal, Department of Economics and Management, University of Helsinki, Finland

Joshua Hurtado Hurtado, Department of Economics and Management, University of Helsinki, Finland

Jessica Jungell-Michelsson, Department of Economics and Management, University of Helsinki, Finland

Andrew P. Kach, Willamette University, USA

Gyöngyi Kovács, HUMLOG Institute, Hanken School of Economics, Helsinki, Finland

Annachiara Longoni, ESADE Business School, Spain

Davide Luzzini, EADA Business School, Spain

Lee Matthews, The International Centre for Corporate Social Responsibility, University of Nottingham, UK

Janne Mende, Max Planck Institute for Comparative Public Law and International Law, Germany

Steve New, Saïd Business School and Hertford College, University of Oxford, UK

Tina Nyfors, Department of Economics and Management, University of Helsinki, Finland

Mark Pagell, University College Dublin, Ireland

Mehrdokht Pournader, University of Melbourne, Australia

Jarkko Pyysiäinen, Department of Economics and Management, University of Helsinki, Finland

Jenny Rinkinen, Department of Social Sciences, LUT University, Finland; Center for Consumer Society Research, University of Helsinki, Finland

Toni Ruuska, Department of Economics and Management, University of Helsinki, Finland

Heini Salonen, Department of Economics and Management, University of Helsinki, Finland

Christoph Scherrer, University of Kassel, Germany

Minelle E. Silva, Asper School of Business, University of Manitoba, Canada

Milla Suomalainen, Department of Economics and Management, University of Helsinki, Finland

Mike Wasserman, Münster School of Business, FH Münster, Germany

Andreas Wieland, Department of Operations Management, Copenhagen Business School, Denmark

Frank Wiengarten, ESADE Business School, Spain

PART I

Diagnosing the crisis

1. The supply chain in crisis

Andreas Wieland and Stefan Gold

1.1 INTRODUCTIONS

For several decades, supply chains have been representatives of the predominant way of organizing the global economy (Kraljic, 1983). It has been noted that 'one of the most significant paradigm shifts of modern business management is that individual businesses no longer compete as solely autonomous entities, but rather as supply chains' (Lambert and Cooper, 2000, p. 65). Due to their focus on the outsourcing of non-core competencies to specialized suppliers of goods and services, and on exploiting comparative cost advantages between regions and countries, supply chains have proven to be extremely powerful systems for generating responsiveness and efficiency in serving customers and consumers. The notion of supply chains as economic powerhouses was complemented by their promise to balance interregional inequality and foster human development around the globe by bringing foreign direct investments and employment opportunities to less developed areas (Abebe et al., 2022).

At the same time, labor supply chains have fueled and steered interregional and international migration and helped provide workers and their families with the opportunity to move up on the social ladder; simultaneously, they provide flexibility to businesses in fulfilling their labor needs (Lai and Baum, 2005). Major geo-political disruptions due to the fall of the iron curtain were key preconditions that supply chains for goods and labor could develop their powerful global reach. Since the 1990s, societies, culture and business—in an intertwined manner—have been increasingly globalized, which was driven by a wave of liberalisation, economic deregulation and reduction of trade barriers, as well as the surge of information and communication technologies and cheap intercontinental transportation through container ships (Lund-Thomsen and Lindgreen, 2014).

The period from the end of the Cold War in the 1990s to the turn of the millennium was characterized by sparking optimism that economic wealth and well-being can reach the most remote places on earth and in societies (i.e., the so-called 'base of the pyramid'; Prahalad, 2005), and that humankind, for the first time in history, can eventually tackle the major challenges regarding hunger, poverty, education, gender equality, health and environmental protection. The eight Millennium Development Goals launched by the United Nations in the year 2000 reflected this optimism. In an era of neo-liberal political predominance, human development targets were closely connected to the idea of unhampered market forces (Held, 2005) that yield a profit even to far-off regions through the distribution mechanism of worldwide trade and supply chains that coordinate this trade.

Outsourcing has been a driver of enormous efficiency gains and mass-market penetration for many goods. This means that also poor consumer groups, at least in the industrialized world, could participate in mass consumption and thus fuel ongoing industrial growth. For example, outsourcing of garment manufacturing to South-East and Southern Asian countries allowed for very low-cost production that makes clothes accessible to large consumer groups, and permits ever accelerating fashion seasons in the frame of fast fashion (Papamichael et al., 2022). As another example, international sourcing vastly increases the variety and affordability of many staple and convenience food items (Gold et al., 2017), causing a substantial drop of the income ratio an average household spends on food in many European countries in the second half of the previous century (Statista, 2022). After increasing saturation of the traditional markets, supply chains were increasingly targeted to the new, growing middle classes of emerging countries such as China, and to poor consumer groups at the base of the pyramid (Prahalad, 2005).

1.2   ENVIRONMENTAL CRISES

Despite these various promises and selective successes of supply chains as economic powerhouses of wealth generation and consumer satisfaction, long-term collateral damage turned out to be devastating. This led to the supply chain being increasingly regarded as a broken system, a mechanism of value destruction rather than value creation. Under applause, images of earth-devouring economic activities of early capitalism had eventually faded away at large in industrialized countries and gave space to the re-emergence of livable human environments and restored ecosystems such as renaturation of formerly brown coalfields. Under the surface, though, supply chains have shifted those images and related economic activities—basically unchanged— to far-off places, bringing their resource-extracting techniques to perfection; and even multiplying their adverse effects on non-renewable resources, biodiversity and climate warming.

Not only do supply chains follow the inert logic of identifying actors and places with best production conditions. Economically speaking, these are often places were environmental degradation are externalities and related costs are not borne by business. This has been observed to lead to a 'race to the bottom' regarding environmental standards and regulation for attracting foreign direct investment and getting connected to global supply chains (Santos and Forte, 2021). The very phenomenon of globally dispersed supply chains does also incur environmental costs due to the necessity of transporting materials, goods and semi-finished products. Trucks, trains, container ships and aircraft are common ways of shipping pre-products between the value-adding supply chain stages.

With all the efficiency and responsiveness thinking in supply chain management (SCM) research and practice, the obvious seems to have been overlooked: that practically all human-made emissions occur along global supply chains and that these supply chain emissions have led the world to the abyss of a climate catastrophe; that the hunger for cheap palm oil and animal feed in our food supply chains has led to monocultures in much of Brazil, Indonesia and Malaysia, the destruction of valuable rainforests and mass extinctions the likes of which we last saw 65 million years ago. Stopping these crises in time would require our immediate and vigorous efforts, but annual additional emissions into the atmosphere continue to tend to increase rather than decrease. All industrial nations consume significantly more global hectares of land along their upstream supply chains than they are entitled to, which means that problems such as deforestation and desertification are becoming an ever-greater problem.

1.3   SOCIAL CRISES

Shifting the burden to far-off or hidden places had also been a common supply chain phenomenon regarding the social pillar of sustainability, where economic activities connected to supply chains have generated labor precarisation and exploitation, as well as adverse effects on community well-being. The Rana Plaza disaster in the Bangladeshi garment industry in 2013 that caused more than a thousand fatalities has epitomized the highly unjust distribution of risks and rewards in international supply chains. Although labor governance systems have been revised in the aftermath of the disaster (Frenkel et al., 2022), improvement has been frustratingly slow on a global scale, and events such as the Covid-19 pandemic or civil wars have caused tough set-backs regarding the position of workers in supply chains (Trautrims et al., 2020). In some instances, the environmental and social side of sustainability are tightly but intricately connected, so that environmental degradation may hint to labor rights violations and, in particular, its extreme form, modern slavery (Bales, 2016).

This may offer new chances for technologically driven supervision and governance of global supply chains (McGrath et al., 2021), for example, through the use of satellite imagery. However, social atrocities in supply chains hidden under the roofs of factories and houses—such as in the form of forced domestic services—cannot be tracked by remote sensing or similar technologies, and might persist as mute islands of social distress and unlawfulness even within affluent societies. The recent debate on modern slavery in supply chains has revealed that SCM research has unduly focused on supply chains of goods and product-service-systems, thereby neglecting labor supply chains (New, 2015)—that is, the question of how exploitable (and disposable; Bales, 1999) labor is recruited. In this respect, conceptions of supply chain management are often a blunt sword when it comes to issues of human and worker rights violations and need to be sharpened (Soundararajan et al., 2021).

With the emergence of ever more global and longer supply chains through the outsourcing of manufacturing processes, there is a disconnect between the upstream end, where workers risk their health to produce parts, modules and finished goods at the lowest possible labor cost, and the downstream end, where wealthy consumers can benefit from low prices for clothing, electronics and food. Western countries pride themselves on their high social standards, but the trade agreements they have initiated have made it possible for these standards to be trampled in manufacturing markets. After more than four decades of global division of labor along supply chains, these imbalances between the upstream and downstream ends of supply chains are now so ingrained in our thinking that consumers, workers, managers and politicians rarely question them.

1.4   POLITICAL CRISES

After a period of globalization driven by economic deregulation and reduction of trade barriers, as well as communication and transportation technologies (Lund-Thomsen and Lindgreen, 2014), tendencies of de-globalization have manifested in political movements (e.g., Le Pen in France, Trumpism, Brexit) and are accompanied by intensified political struggles for global hegemony. Geopolitical disruptions have exacerbated occurrence of supply chain disruptions and shortages, and have rendered supply chain governance for planetary boundaries and human rights and well-being more complicated (Roscoe et al., 2020). Supply chains are increasingly fragmented between power blocs and are threatened not only through attacks (e.g., cyber attacks; Luo and Choi, 2022) but also a new wave of armed political conflicts.

The political problems associated with the fact that we organize our global economy through supply chains are often identified as supply chain-related problems only on closer inspection because of the complexity of the overall context. Supply chain thinking can then be identified as the trigger for a multifaceted avalanche: workers in the West are losing their jobs because of the outsourcing of manufacturing processes; job loss leads to income inequality and poverty; parts of the former working class are driven into the arms of populists who promise a quick fix with simple narratives and identify migrants as scapegoats; and, in the end, politicians promise that the nation-state and its economic closure to other markets will be the solution, as we have seen in the case of Brexit and the US-China trade war—phenomena that ultimately threatened the prosperity of entire countries even further.

In other words: Both academic research on global supply chains and corporate practice have often ignored these broader connections. Textbooks on SCM have attempted to prioritize business success in terms of profits and cost reductions. The often-unintended political consequences of 'successful' (from a short-term perspective of a single firm) SCM have been relegated to other disciplines (e.g., political science) and decision-makers (e.g., government agencies). One reason for overlooking these consequences is linear thinking. For decades, SCM research has tried to test cause-and-effect relationships between a few variables instead of understanding the complex overall context. Rather than exploring or even developing new grand narratives, this type of thinking has often resulted in irrelevant propositions or hypotheses. Variables that were not part of the model, often political ones, remained hidden. Even worse, many supply chain managers have argued that what they read in our academic journals is useless for their professional reality.

1.5   INTERCONNECTEDNESS OF CRISES

On closer inspection, it is not sufficient to look at such crises in isolation. Many crises are complex, and they are in many ways intertwined with global supply chains. For example, the outsourcing of manufacturing processes has made many problems invisible to Western consumers: Environmental pollution and social problems now occur geographically far from the consumer's own perception and are not linked to own consumption patterns any longer. Only by undermining minimum environmental and social standards in developing countries has it become possible to produce goods at the price levels consumers are used to today. Raising these standards in producer markets will certainly alleviate some of today's crises, but at the same time could raise costs in consumer markets and, as a result, might lead to political crises.

Political crises can quickly affect supply chains. Shortly after the Russian attack on Ukraine, Western European automakers quickly ran out of certain key components that were produced in Ukraine. Ukraine is also an important market for agricultural producers, so the war affected global grain and other food supplies. In such cases, the disruption of supply chains due to political crises can quickly lead to an intensification of social crises. For example, some African countries, which are already particularly affected by the climate crisis, depend on grain supplies from Ukraine and Russia. This is another example of the complexity of global crises. While the supply chain is the focus of this example, optimising it in isolation would not be effective without considering the political, environmental and social issues that affect it. The interdependence of these crises creates a dilemma that can only be resolved by taking a holistic view.

1.6   A WAY FORWARD: SYSTEMIC AND HOLISTIC THINKING

The multi-causality, interconnectedness and recursive relation of supply chain related sustainability issues—on the ecological, social, or economic side—often qualify those as 'wicked problems' (Rittel and Webber, 1973) or 'grand challenges' (George et al., 2016) for which there are no easy and straightforward solutions. This means that multi-actor solutions are required, for example, in the sense of issue-focused stakeholder management (Roloff, 2008), which is directed towards addressing moral causes (i.e., issues such as poverty or environmental pollution) and may be initiated but not dominated by corporations. For a holistic grasp of supply chains, they have to be re-conceptualized as both objective and socially constructed entities (Gold, 2014) that operate in a complex economic system and are embedded in broader socio-cultural, as well as ecological, environments in a dynamic interactive way (Wieland, 2021).

Technological developments in recent years are paving the way for a new kind of quantitative research: Instead of correlating a handful of variables in a structural equation model, we now have algorithms at hand that are able to connect millions of pieces of data to find patterns. This has opened the door to a kind of research that can quantitatively capture the complexity of our world. In particular, developments in artificial intelligence are challenging the traditions of quantitative research at a breathtaking pace. Interestingly, the procedures and results of this research follow an exploratory rationale, and hence often resemble qualitative rather than quantitative thinking. If our doctoral programs, journal guidelines, and research practices do not adapt to these developments in time, the discipline will become obsolete, leaving the field of research to a small number of American and Chinese IT giants that store data and are able to analyze them. Commercial interests rather than freedom of research for the good of the world would be the result.

Qualitative research also needs to find a new role. It should be noted here that in recent years SCM research has rarely explicitly defined itself as social science research. Yet, this would be important: Who, if not a social science, could give new meaning to the world by critically questioning old truths? It is actually quite obvious that in a complex world, there exists no single truth that could ever be traced in a positivist way. However, questioning traditional assumptions requires a normative element in SCM research that has been largely absent until now. It has often even been said that 'researchers must be neutral'. As a result, SCM research has tended to theorize as a camera of existing rather than an engine of possible solutions. If it is willing to abandon this dogma of neutrality, the opportunity for future SCM research lies in developing new, better narratives that would take into account planetary boundaries, workers' rights, democratic freedoms, humanism and cultural diversity. SCM research would then shift from small-scale theory building and testing to large-scale theory imagination.

1.7   ANOTHER WAY FORWARD: TRANSFORMATIVE PUBLIC POLICY

Notwithstanding encouraging developments regarding business voluntarily taking on a lead role in transforming supply chains towards greater sustainability and thus becoming value generation engines in a broader sense (i.e., embracing social, environmental and economic value) (e.g., Pagell and Wu, 2009; Sunar and Swaminathan, 2022), many firms prioritize profits over value-based principles such as working conditions or the reduction of environmental externalities (Montabon et al., 2016). For changing the rules of the game of supply chains, public policy is a largely neglected but important element of a sustainability transformation (Bodrožić and Gold, 2024). The Covid-19 pandemic (2020–2022) has highlighted the significance of governments, states and inter-governmental bodies such as the World Health Organization (WHO) to take on an active and leading role in tackling the crisis. Pucker (2022) has pointed out that public policy may change how firms prioritize sustainability-related issues in their operational and strategic decision-making. Leading supply chains out of crisis will require going decisively beyond laissez-faire public policy that principally focusses on mitigating market failures (Laplane and Mazzucato, 2020). Regulatory approaches (e.g., UK Modern Slavery Act or the German Supply Chain Due Diligence Law) have to be strengthened and beyond this, a transformative public policy may be necessary to navigate economies and societies through the troubled water of the current period of crisis (Schumpeter, 1942). An extended period of economic and social instability has started with the dot-com crash (in 2000), continued with the financial crisis (in 2008/2009) and still persists today. A transformative public policy orchestrates programs ('missions'; Mazzucato, 2021) and creates knowledge and infrastructure ('systems') so to facilitate private industry, investment and society to move the modus operandi of supply chains towards desirable sustainability (Bodrožić and Gold, 2024).

REFERENCES

Abebe, G., McMillan, M., & Serafinelli, M. (2022). Foreign direct investment and knowledge diffusion in poor locations. *Journal of Development Economics*, 158, 102926.

Bales, K. (1999). *Disposable people: New slavery in the global economy*. University of California Press.

Bales, K. (2016). *Blood and earth: Modern slavery, ecocide, and the secret to saving the world*. Random House.

Bodrožić, Z., & Gold, S. (2024). Building diverse, equitable, and inclusive operations and supply chains: Bringing public policy back in. *Production and Operations Management*, doi: 10.1177/10591478241229077.

Frenkel, S.J., Rahman, S., & Rahman, K.M. (2022). After Rana Plaza: Governing exploitative workplace labour regimes in Bangladeshi garment export factories. *Journal of Industrial Relations*, 64(2), 272-297.

George, G., Howard-Grenville, J., Joshi, A., & Tihanyi, L. (2016). Understanding and tackling societal grand challenges through management research. *Academy of Management Journal*, 59(6), 1880-1895.

Gold, S. (2014). Supply chain management as Lakatosian research program. *Supply Chain Management: International Journal*, 19(1), 1-9.

Gold, S., Kunz, N., & Reiner, G. (2017). Sustainable global agrifood supply chains: Exploring the barriers. *Journal of Industrial Ecology*, 21(2), 249-260.

Held, D. (2005). Toward a new consensus: Answering the dangers of globalization. *Harvard International Review*, 27(2), 14-17.

Kraljic, P. (1983). Purchasing must become supply management. *Harvard Business Review*, 61, 109-117.

Lai, P.-C., & Baum, T. (2005). Just-in-time labour supply in the hotel sector: The role of agencies. *Employee Relations*, 27(1), 86-102.

Lambert, D.M., & Cooper, M.C. (2000). Issues in supply chain management. *Industrial Marketing Management*, 29(1), 65-83.

Laplane, A.M., & Mazzucato, M. (2020). Socializing the risks and rewards of public investments: Economic, policy, and legal issues. *Research Policy*, 49, 100008.

Lund-Thomsen, P., & Lindgreen, A. (2014). Corporate social responsibility in global value chains: Where are we now and where are we going? *Journal of Business Ethics*, 123(1), 11-22.

Luo, S., & Choi, T.-M. (2022). E-commerce supply chains with considerations of cyber-security: Should governments play a role? *Production and Operations Management*, 31(5), 2107-2126.

Mazzucato, M. (2021). *Mission economy: A moonshot guide to changing capitalism*. Penguin UK.

McGrath, P., McCarthy, L., Marshall, D., & Rehme, J. (2021). Tools and technologies of transparency in sustainable global supply chains. *California Management Review*, 64(1), 67-89.

Montabon, F., Pagell, M., & Wu, Z. (2016). Making sustainability sustainable. *Journal of Supply Chain Management*, 52(2), 11-27.

New, S.J. (2015). Modern slavery and the supply chain: The limits of corporate social responsibility? *Supply Chain Management: An International Journal*, 20, 697-707.

Pagell, M., & Wu, Z. (2009). Building a more complete theory of sustainable supply chain management using case studies of 10 exemplars. *Journal of Supply Chain Management*, 45(2), 37-56.

Papamichael, I., Chatziparaskeva, G., Pedreño, J.N., Voukkali, I., Almendro Candel, M.B., & Zorpas, A.A. (2022). Building a new mind set in tomorrow fashion development through circular strategy models in the framework of waste management. *Current Opinion in Green and Sustainable Chemistry*, 36, 100638.

Prahalad, C.K. (2005). *The fortune at the bottom of the pyramid*. Wharton School Publishing.

Pucker, K.P. (2022, 13 January). The myth of sustainable fashion. *Harvard Business Review*. https://hbr.org/2022/01/the-myth-of-sustainable-fashion

Rittel, H.W.J., & Webber, M.M. (1973). Dilemmas in a general theory of planning. *Policy Sciences*, 4(2), 155-169.

Roloff, J. (2008). Learning from multi-stakeholder networks: Issue-focused stakeholder management. *Journal of Business Ethics*, 82, 233–250.

Roscoe, S., Skipworth, H., Aktas, E., & Habib, F. (2020). Managing supply chain uncertainty arising from geopolitical disruptions: Evidence from the pharmaceutical industry and Brexit. *International Journal of Operations & Production Management*, 40(9), 1499-1529.

Santos, A., & Forte, R. (2021). Environmental regulation and FDI attraction: A bibliometric analysis of the literature. *Environmental Science and Pollution Research*, 28(7), 8873-8888.

Schumpeter, J.A. (1942). *Capitalism, socialism, and democracy*. Harper & Row.

Soundararajan, V., Wilhelm, M.M., & Crane, A. (2021). Humanizing research on working conditions in supply chains: Building a path to decent work. *Journal of Supply Chain Management*, 57(2), 3-13.

Statista. (2022). Share of total income spent on basic essentials, such as food and clothing, in the European Union in 1950 and the 1990s. https://www.statista.com/statistics/1073153/share-income-spent-basics-eu-1950-1990s/

Sunar, N., & Swaminathan, J.M. (2022). Socially relevant and inclusive operations management. *Production and Operations Management*, 31(12), 4379-4392.

Trautrims, A., Schleper, M.C., Cakir, M.S., & Gold, S. (2020). Survival at the expense of the weakest? Managing modern slavery risks in supply chains during COVID-19. *Journal of Risk Research*, 23(7-8), 1067-1072.

Wieland, A. (2021). Dancing the supply chain: Toward transformative supply chain management. *Journal of Supply Chain Management*, 57(1), 58–73.

2. Supplying the Anthropocene: cultural turning in process

Pasi Heikkurinen, Toni Ruuska, Johanna Hohenthal, Jenny Rinkinen, Jarkko Pyysiäinen, Joshua Hurtado Hurtado, Jessica Jungell-Michelsson, Heini Salonen, Tina Nyfors and Milla Suomalainen

2.1 INTRODUCTION

Supply chains shape the world. They are also integral to the processes of expansive consumption and extraction of natural resources, as well as for production of emissions and handling of waste. While the awareness of human cultures' influence on matter-energetic processes dates as far back as to the previous century, the observation that humankind has become a force of nature is based on new geological evidence. And since there are now signs of human doings and negative anthropogenic impacts on ecosystems everywhere on Earth—air, land, and water—and beyond, the Anthropocene Working Group (Zalasiewicz et al., 2017) of the International Commission on Stratigraphy has proposed a new epoch in the geologic time scale.

This new epoch, the Anthropocene, is claimed to be distinct from its predecessor, the Holocene, in terms of Earth system functioning. In the Anthropocene, '[h]umanity itself has become a global geophysical force', significantly influencing the operation of the biosphere (Steffen et al., 2011, p. 741; see also Crutzen and Stoermer, 2000; Crutzen, 2002). The scale and impact of humans on the planet is so vast that the climate is found to be perilously changing, biodiversity is recorded to be rapidly decreasing, and the ocean levels are on a severe rise. We call this development 'the ecospheric crisis'—a planetary catastrophe not limited to the undesired consequences on the biotic life—and take the Anthropocene concept as its symbol, as it empirically points out the ubiquitous impact of human culture on ecosystems.

If we look at the anatomy of the ecospheric crisis, it is certainly plausible to argue for the reduction of consumption and production (Kallis, 2018; Kallis et al., 2020; Hickel, 2021). The increasing demand for earthbound resources, and in particular their extraction, processing, transport, and manufacture to maintain the global growth-based economy has led, and continues to lead, to a destruction of local livelihoods, indigenous ways of life, and creates havoc on a plenitude of non-human (wild) habitats. Waste, emissions, pollution, and habitat destruction again lead to environmental change, of which perhaps the most notable is global warming, and the resulting climate change (Steffen, Richardson et al., 2015; IPCC, 2022). These changes in the environment in turn accelerate biodiversity loss (Barnosky et al., 2012; Steffen, Broadgate et al., 2015), as species are unable to adapt to the human-made transformations in their life worlds.

In this chapter, we portray supply chains as undergoing a systemic crisis because of frequent disruptions caused by political conflicts and the ecospheric crisis: for instance, the Covid-19 pandemic, climate change, and other reasons for resource shortages (Mitchell et al., 2020). Further, we argue that supply chains are also inherently linked to causing such crises, which have visibly cumulated as 'the Anthropocene' (e.g., Heikkurinen et al., 2016; Arboleda, 2020). To understand why this is so, let us look at the global economy through a relational lens (Heikkurinen et al., 2021) as an organism consisting of several organs, which are connected by veins. The supply chains act as those veins connecting one organ to another, enabling the whole organism to grow and progress. Not only are they energy-consuming sources of material inputs, but also highly cognitive and normative systems having practical repercussions by delivering products and information, as well as other less tangible products.

The cognitive, normative, and practical aspects and implications of global supply chains can be further unpacked with the help of the concepts of culture and cultural practices—the idea of a cultural turn regarding the analysis of supply chains. From a cultural point of view, it makes no sense to merely talk about a single, monolithic social construct of 'global supply chains', even if we could analytically abstract some important operational principles characteristic of supply chains globally. Instead, it proves more fruitful and illuminating to treat supply chains themselves as a set of cultures, or practices having normative rationalities embedded in cultures. Therefore, we focus here on analyzing the processes whereby supply-chains-as-practices become (to various degrees) embedded in local cultural orders, practices, and place-based sociocultural relations. We suggest that these sociocultural relations variably align, reinforce, conflict with, or resign to the practices and rationalities of (global) supply chains.

In the ecospheric crisis, where the overuse and misuse of resources and the over-sized and perpetual growth of the global economy produce the emergency (Bonnedahl and Heikkurinen, 2019; Bonnedahl et al. 2022), supply chains cannot be detached from the generative sources and dynamics of the crisis. Instead, supply chains are found in a processual relation with multiple causes and effects pertaining to the crisis as a whole. Whilst this may be a radical statement from a neoclassical economics point of view, things complicate even further when the cultural variable is introduced. In other words, the multiple causes and their cascading effects (Pescaroli and Alexander, 2016, 2018) are always culture-laden, situated in a cultural fabric—also in the case of a seemingly decontextualized Anthropocene narrative. One entry point to the notion of culture in relation to the supply chain literature and the Anthropocene debate can be made through the so-called consumerist culture encouraging citizens to become global consumers and requiring a well-functioning global supply of goods and services.

In this chapter, we aim to make a case for a greater 'cultural sensitivity'—by which we mean not only acceptance towards the diversity of cultures, but particularly paying attention to the relevance of 'culture', as well as taking the implications of this 'turning' into account—in organizing the anthropogenic supply of goods and services. We do so by first shortly commenting on the interdisciplinary Anthropocene debate, explicating the connection between global supply chains and the Anthropocene epoch (Section 2). Secondly, following Fine and Leopold (1993), as well as Fine et al. (2018), we conceptualize the supply chain as an integrated system of provision (Section 3). We further embed the global supply chains to capitalism, characterizing it as having roots in colonial-era power relations and taking advantage of the world's poor (Section 4). In the final part of this chapter, we discuss how a cultural turn could manifest in the study of supply chains in crisis, and lead to gaining a better understanding of how different lenses to the claimed Anthropocene (crisis) may connect to one another in each spatiotemporal context. Such an understanding can lead to finding ways towards sustainability in the new epoch.

2.2   THE SCIENCES OF THE ANTHROPOCENE

A little over 20 years after its introduction, the Anthropocene concept is widely used but also widely contested and debated (see, e.g., Heikkurinen, 2017; Heikkurinen et al., 2019). After the atmospheric chemist Paul Crutzen and his colleague Eugene F. Stoermer, a leading researcher in diatoms, coined the term, several biologists, ecologists, and paleontologists have rushed to support their findings. Not all scientists, however, have been equally satisfied with this idea of the 'geology of mankind' (Crutzen and Stoermer, 2000). Most notably, the Anthropocene concept has received fierce critique from the social sciences and humanities, and consequently, there are now competing diagnoses of the crisis. Terms like Capitalocene (Moore, 2014), Chthulucene (Haraway, 2015), Ecocene (Küpers, 2020), Humilocene (Abram et al., 2020), Manthropocene

(Hultman and Pulé, 2019), Nafthocene (Vadén, 2021), Plutocene (Ulvila and Wilén, 2017), Negrocene (Ferdinand et al., 2020), Paxcene (Heikkurinen, 2019), and Technocene (Hornborg, 2015) are all reactions to the concept of the Anthropocene. Significantly for our analysis, they all place blame differently and call for different actions to respond to the ongoing crisis. While some terms are more forward-looking, in the sense that they are already seeking to imagine a time after the Anthropocene, others remain more critical in terms of diagnosing what the root causes of the new epoch are. As a whole, however, these alternative conceptions to the Anthropocene share a tendency to reveal various cultural tenets related to the crisis.

While there are empirical grounds to argue for an epochal shift in the Earth system (e.g., Waters et al., 2016), and make the case that these changes are largely anthropogenic (Steffen et al., 2007; Steffen, Broadgate et al., 2015), at the same time, it holds true that humanity cannot be limited to a single collective agent. That is, there are so many kinds of humans and not all are equally accountable. Indeed, a paradox is in-built in the name of the proposed new epoch: the 'human' epoch. Although human beings—not other mammals, or fish, reptiles, or birds—have forcibly affected the earth system and pushed ecosystems towards tipping points, or even to a verge of collapse (Newbold et al., 2015; Hansen and Stone, 2016), not all of them are responsible for these occurrences (e.g., Malm and Hornborg, 2014; Baskin, 2015; Moore, 2015; Ulvila and Wilén, 2017; Bauer and Ellis, 2018; Barca, 2020). It is rather clear that the sternest attack from various strands of critical social sciences targets the universalizing and standardizing effect of the Anthropocene term, and the potential harm this kind of narrative and historical interpretation may imply (e.g., Moore, 2015; Simpson, 2018; Swyngedouw and Ernstson, 2018).

Although the critiques raise important issues, and clearly also point out the shortcomings of the Anthropocene term, they cannot water down the stratigraphical evidence, on rocks and rock layering, on the planet. That is, the empirical grounds for proposing a new geological epoch are sound. This geological epoch results from the global operations of a single species, although very asymmetrically, to the Earth system. Therefore, there is factual basis to call the new geological epoch the Anthropocene. At the same time, this naturalizing finding should be complemented with a cultural understanding—something social sciences and humanities could offer, for instance, shedding light on the role of different historical interpretations on socio-economic inequalities (Heikkurinen et al., 2019; Heikkurinen et al., 2020). We hence propose that only a combined and balanced portrayal of the epoch and its relations to human cultures (including critical discourses) can provide a sufficient understanding of the crisis which supply chains have (partially) provoked and in which they are embedded.

2.3 GLOBAL SUPPLY CHAINS AS SYSTEMS OF PROVISIONING

When seeking to make sense of the human operations that have pushed, and continue to push, ecosystems and the climate towards a state shift (Barnosky et al. 2012), we should pay more attention to the processes of global supply chains. Following Fine and Leopold (1993), as well as Fine et al. (2018), the supply chain is conceptualized here as an integrated system of provision: a logistics and production system that encompasses activities, such as land use, extraction, processing, smelting, transporting, manufacturing, wholesaling, retailing, consumption, and use, including reuse from the so-called waste. This view encompasses the full chain of activities underpinning the material production and cultural significance of different goods. Industrial supply chains are also dependent and closely interlinked with the 'planetary mine,' a global system of extraction, logistics, and processing (Arboleda, 2020). As Arboleda (2020, p. 5) argues, 'geographies of extraction have become entangled in a global apparatus of production and exchange'. With this, we want to stress the increasing integration of the world economy, and the integral role of supply chains in sustaining the prevailing levels of production and consumption, whilst at the same time paying attention to the context-specific determinants of any instances of production and consumption (Fine et al., 2018).

Furthermore, supply chains in various forms have served trade for as long as it has existed, but in the contemporary world, they are a distinctive feature of the global capitalist economy. In her work, Anna Tsing (2009, pp. 148–149) uses the term 'supply chain capitalism' to describe the large-scale commodity chains relying on subcontracting possibilities that have enabled outsourcing; it has been hailed as a key to efficiency and cost reduction. Thus, according to Tsing (2009), those who benefit from global supply chains are primarily the large corporations that participate in the extractive industries, transportation, and manufacturing, as well as the developers of new technologies and financial arrangements that enable the outsourcing.

It is the global supply chains that guarantee the availability of a wide variety of relatively cheap products for the wealthy consumers (LeBaron and Lister, 2021) mainly through a few giant retailers and branded merchandisers (Biénabe et al., 2007; Chan et al., 2013). On the one hand, these chains create employment opportunities, particularly in manufacturing, transportation, storage, and distribution sectors in the Global South. On the other hand, the sourcing and purchasing practices of global buyers, and the rationalized supply chain management techniques, are designed to enhance efficiency in the global 'just-in-time' sourcing and production, which are associated with labor violations (Lee, 2016). The global supply chains also threaten local economies via contributing to small producers' difficulties entering the market due to high quality standards and/or inability to compete with the low prices of the giant retailers (Vorley et al., 2007).

In the culture of global capitalism (e.g., Mészáros, 2010; Robinson, 2014), the developments in logistics, transport and communications facilitate dispersal of economic activity across the Earth—to a larger and larger geographical space (Harvey, 2014). Arboleda (2020) complements these observations by claiming that in the 21st century a new geography of late industrialization persists. It is no longer the West that is the heartland of capitalism, but East Asia and the Pacific region has emerged as an important capitalist territory. According to Arboleda (2020), the global supply chains are tied together by robotization and computerization. Smart and increasingly automated supply chains are the backbone of industrialized modern way of life. They organize and enable the hectic and fragmented urbanization, and objectify 'unspectacular, nearly imperceptible practices and habits that constantly weave together the fabric of everyday life in the twenty-first century city: sending an email, driving to work, ordering groceries from the internet' (Arboleda, 2020, p. 13).

The supply chain in the global context is analogous to and dependent on the processes of capital; they both seek to survive and grow (Edwards, 2017; Ruuska, 2021). And as interdisciplinary Anthropocene sciences witness, this largely happens at the expense of natural habitats and diversity, labor conditions, and human rights. The global supply chain is the system where the provisioning of capital and technology meet: through capitalist markets, supply chains internalize raw materials, energy, and other supplies into the form of production lines, logistics, and management. Moreover, Edwards (2017) notes that the supply chain internalizes, molds, and moves resources, as it externalizes waste and valueless matter all over its global reach. In contrast to the processes of the biosphere, which sustain diversity, capital feeds the global supply chain, which is toxic and destructive towards many kinds of processes—not least the matter-energetic flow on Earth—that ultimately also sustain its own functioning.

The environmental and cultural impacts resulting from global supply chains in a constantly expanding and growing world economy become staggering. One of the most prominent measurements and illustrations of these impacts on the human socio-economic spheres, and on the Earth system, is the work by Steffen, Broadgate, and colleagues (2015). In their 'trajectory of the Anthropocene' that is called 'The Great Acceleration' (which began in 1950, and continues to this day—a period that roughly coincides with the existence of global supply chains and the era of globalization)—they first present the socio-economic trends of that period.

These socio-economic trends follow the so-called hockey stick curve shape, signifying exponential growth. This is no coincidence, since almost all nations and international organizations aim for, at least, 3% annual growth in GDP (e.g., Kallis et al. 2020; Hickel 2021). The 70-year exponential growth in aggregate socio-economic factors has impacted the ecosphere on such a scale that humans have become a force of nature with destabilizing and catastrophic consequences. On this, Steffen, Broadgate et al. (2015, p. 92) conclude, as follows:

> The socio-economic Great Acceleration graphs [...] clearly show the phenomenal growth of the human enterprise after the Second World War, both in economic activity, and hence consumption, and in resource use. The corresponding Earth System graphs [...] also show significant changes in rates or states of all parameters in the 20th century, although a mid-century sharp acceleration is not so clearly defined in all of them. Nevertheless, the coupling between the two sets of 12 graphs is striking. Correlation in time does not prove cause-and-effect, of course, but there is a vast amount of evidence that the changes in the structure and functioning of the Earth System shown in Figure 3 are primarily driven by human activities.

They add that although the figures do not necessarily indicate that the current state of the Earth System is different from the Holocene, there 'is convincing evidence that the parameters have moved well outside of the Holocene envelope of variability' (Steffen, Richardson et al., 2015), signifying a shift to a new geological epoch. Another telling finding of the human impact on Earth is a study by Elhacham et al. (2020), which argues that the global human-made mass of buildings, roads, infrastructure, and commodities now exceeds all living biomass. Thus, in the Anthropocene, the Earth is full of humans, the things of affluent humans, and the waste and pollution originating from the production and consumption of those things. Worse still, the number of humans, their stuff, and the amount of waste and pollution continues to grow.

2.4   EMBEDDING SUPPLY IN THE CRISIS

The political analyses of supply chain disruptions often consider only the immediate disastrous events, systemic errors and accidents causing the disruptions. This can be seen to divert the attention away from the 'world order of competition in which the economy is more important than life, including that of the human species' (Mignolo, 2020, p. 212). Such a rather weak and culturally simplistic logic fails to see the vulnerabilities inherent in the capitalist system, in which 'the effect is the cause' (Fanon, 1961, p. 45; see also Mignolo, 2020).

The major problems of the global supply chain (including its vulnerability) are fundamentally based on its embeddedness in the cycles of raw-materials, fuels, and labor. These cycles depend heavily on two things that can be considered inherent to our consumerist culture: the persistent colonial-era power relations (Bhambra, 2021) and the intersecting disadvantages of workers (Tsing, 2009). The first dependency is well illustrated by two grand interlinked disasters of the Anthropocene: climate change and biodiversity loss. The frequent extreme weather events and the rising sea levels associated with climate change significantly impact food production, natural resource extraction, and transportation, and have cascading impacts on other sectors through the global supply chain network (Ghadge et al., 2020). However, global supply chains contribute to climate change, for example, through greenhouse gas emissions (Ghadge et al., 2020). Furthermore, extractive operations, such as oil drilling, mining, and logging, serve both fossil and 'green' industries (e.g., renewable energy production; Dunlap and Brock, 2022). Together with the warming climate, these extractive operations have adverse impacts on ecosystems and biodiversity.

Biodiversity crises have been called 'business crises' because raw material and product supply depends on various ecosystem services such as carbon sequestration, air purification, and the provision of raw materials, food, genetic, and medicinal resources (Kurth et al., 2021). However, less attention has been given to the equally important fact that the extractive industries often operate on and damage the living areas of Indigenous people and other marginalized groups whose cultures and ways of living are closely tied to local environments (see e.g., Gudynas, 2019; Koenig, 2020). This land and resource grabbing is enabled by the prevailing colonial matrix of power that emerged with the colonization of the Americas around the year 1500 and Africa in the 19th century and coincided with the accelerated spread of the capitalist world order (Amin, 1993; Quijano, 2000; Mignolo, 2007; Polanyi Levitt, 2014; Patel and Moore, 2017; Mignolo, 2018, 2020).

The second dependency became visible during a recent global crisis, the Covid-19 pandemic. The pandemic disrupted the availability of labor, a critical resource for different supply chain network activities, such as production, transportation, storage, and distribution (Stephens et al., 2020; Nagurney, 2021). This labor, however, consists of workers whose economic performance and contracts are tied to cultural factors often excluded from the realm of economy, such as gender, race, ethnicity, and age. These very same factors establish the 'super-exploitation' of workers (i.e., exploitation depending on the abovementioned factors, which is greater than exploitation that might be expected from general economic principles) and affect class formation (Tsing, 2009). The evidence from intersectional analyses shows that marginalized people, particularly people of color in low-income classes, who are essential workers in supply chain activities, have been disproportionally exposed to the coronavirus and have less access to health care than other social groups (Obinna, 2021). Often, they also live in areas with high exposure to environmental health risks caused by the production and transportation activities linked to supply chains (Sasser et al., 2021). Therefore, as supply chain capitalism depends on the labor, its crisis is also driven by the intersecting vulnerabilities of its workers.

The root causes of the environmental and social damage of the global supply chain have so far not been properly addressed through sustainable supply chain solutions, despite the notion that some advances in corporate social responsibility (CSR) initiatives, industry-wide programs, and multi-stakeholder initiatives have arguably been made (Brock and Dunlap, 2018; LeBaron and Lister, 2021). This may be related to the inherent paradox of supply chain capitalism: while the coloniality of power and global injustices underlie the supply chain crises, it is also in the interest of the capitalist system to sustain them (Harvey, 2014). Supply chain management is subordinate to the narrative of modernity that claims capitalist economic progress and growth to be for the benefit of everyone. Such 'promises of modernity legitimize coloniality, that is, oppression, exploitation, and dispossession' (Mignolo, 2018, p. 145). This interconnection, however, cannot be made explicit without running against the promises of modernity (Mignolo, 2018), which makes the decolonial analysis of supply chain management unappealing within the capitalist system.

Political conflicts and war are also phenomena fed by global supply chains. At the same time, global supply chains suffer disruptions because of them. For example, Healy et al. (2019) attribute responsibility to the fossil fuel industry for both generating chains of energy injustices along the transboundary fossil fuel supply chains and unintentionally stimulating the rise of trans-local solidarity movements that disrupt those same supply chains. In addition, research from the field of peace and conflict studies link oil dependence to the onset of civil wars, and the production and distribution of gemstones, opium, coca, and cannabis to the duration of intra-state conflicts (Ross, 2004). Herzberg and Lorz (2020), in turn, describe the relationship between global supply chains and conflict in the following terms: 'Firms from the North import natural resources from the South to produce final consumption goods. In one of the countries in the South, local groups attempt to access natural resources, which results in rent-seeking conflicts' (p. 395). This relationship between the (extractive) dynamics of the global supply chain and conflict and war is indicative of the crises of the Anthropocene and the human suffering it produces.

2.5 DISCUSSION AND CONCLUSION

Although we have an increasing understanding of anthropogenic supply processes (e.g., on how humans negatively impact their environment and other co-humans), and we gain this understanding by developing more accurate metrics and transdisciplinary models, we are still largely at odds about who and what in 'humans' are to blame and what to do about it (Heikkurinen et al., 2019). And, even if we were able to draw conclusions on the main drivers and expected consequences of grand phenomena like climate change, the inter-human black box—culture—would remain to be debated. That is, the nature of our understanding is largely processual, calling for a more detailed analysis of a set of perspectives for the diversity of situated phenomena (Nietzsche, [1882–1887] 2001; Gadamer, 1975; Simpson, 2012). We thus argue that different place-based systems of provisioning can be considered examples of these diverse, situated phenomena.

When accounting for greater cultural sensitivity in organizing and managing the anthropogenic supply of goods and services, we want to emphasize two aspects: first, the context-specific determinants of the larger-scale supply chains and second, the integrated nature of production and consumption. The concept of 'systems of provision' is useful here as it characterizes connections between sites of production, distribution, retailing, design, marketing, and final consumption (Fine and Leopold, 1993). Whereas a local system of provision might only involve movement of raw materials and goods from farm to shop to home, a more extended system entails movements of materials, technologies, labor, and goods between different sites of production and processing around the world before reaching the sites of consumption, like our homes.

In both cases, the reconfiguration of practices of provision (such as manufacturing, retailing, and distribution) and consumption (such as shopping and use) is ongoing and intersecting (Rinkinen et al., 2019). Global supply chains may seem to unify 'needs' and doings across different sites, but routines, practices, and related patterns of consumption co-evolve with context-specific systems of planning and infrastructures (Shove and Trentmann, 2018; Rinkinen et al., 2021). To a large extent, demand is made by supply chains and not simply existing and waiting to be met by supply (Rinkinen et al., 2020). This is an important point for understanding the constitutive role of supply chains. In other words, supply chains are not merely in crises but very much also an active site of constituting them. To continue with the previous example of the super-exploitation of health care workers during the coronavirus pandemic: such exploitation is partly due to the status of life ensuring care as a critical societal contract—a rather unnegotiated demand for health care. However, this demand happens largely due to the fact that these facilities and practices exist and are written in the 'societal supply contracts'. This is, of course, a contradictory and sensitive example that does not explain the discrimination and the exploitation of the most vulnerable workers.

Also, as Rinkinen et al. (2019) show, deeply 'cultural' notions such as quality, risk, modernity, safety, and tradition are anchored in the details of supply and provision. Such discourses should therefore not be treated as external drivers of supply but rather seen as embedded in the multiple and intersecting systems of provision, which again—as Gold and Heikkurinen (2013) remark — are finally all embedded in the ecosphere. The cultural aspects of supply chains are enacted at all scales by enactors across the entire system of provisioning and enabled by different processes of the society, economy, and technology, for example (Rinkinen et al., 2019). This can be illustrated, for instance, by looking at the intersections of changing expectations of thermal comfort and developments in heat supply (Watson and Shove, 2022).

For further studies, an example of an analytical frame for studying phenomena—like supply chains, community resilience, or the welfare state—from a culturally sensitive perspective could consist of investigating the enactors, enablers, and enactments in a particular, topically relevant context. Such an analysis could begin by first identifying the culturally relevant enactors, enablers, and enactments. These can be human and nonhuman, as well as more or less material. Secondly, the analysis could proceed to evaluating their degrees of focality for the topic of interest, like social change or product development. The criteria for focality can be defined situationally. In the third phase, the analysis could then proceed to understanding the dynamics (including tensions) between the 'chosen' set—and/or sets—of focal enactors, enablers, and enactments. In a culturally sensitive study, relevant findings may emerge by comparing and contrasting, first, the internal dynamics of a set of enactors, enablers, and enactments that in a particular context form 'a culture' and, second, the external dynamics of that 'culture' towards other cultures, be they parallel or 'host cultures', as well as the border(s) of what is viewed and taken as 'internal' and 'external' (Van Dijk and Rietveld, 2017; Heikkurinen et al., 2021; Pyysiäinen, 2021).

ACKNOWLEDGEMENTS

Heikkurinen, Ruuska, Hohenthal, Pyysiäinen, Suomalainen are funded by Research Council Finland, grant number 343277 (Skills of self-provisioning in rural communities); Rinkinen is funded by Research Council Finland, grant number 333556 (Citizens, Everyday Life and Tensions in the Energy Transition); Hurtado Hurtado is funded by Maj and Tor Nessling Foundation, grant agreement 202200237 (Diverse Economies and Regenerative Cities), Jungell-Michelsson and Salonen are funded by University of Helsinki's Doctoral Programme in Interdisciplinary Environmental Sciences (DENVI); and Nyfors is funded by Tiina and Antti Herlin Foundation.

REFERENCES

Abram, D., Milstein, T., & Castro-Sotomayor, J. (2020). Interbreathing ecocultural identity in the Humilocene. In: Milstein, T., Castro-Sotomayor, J. (eds.), *Routledge handbook of ecocultural identity*, 5–25, Routledge.

Amin, S. (1993). The ancient world-systems versus the modern capitalist world-system. In: Frank, A.G., Gills, B.K. (eds.), *The world system. Five hundred years or five thousand*, 247–277, Routledge, London.

Arboleda, M. (2020). *Planetary mine: Territories of extraction under late capitalism.* Verso Books.

Barca, S. (2020). *Forces of reproduction: Notes for a counter-hegemonic Anthropocene.* Cambridge University Press.

Barnosky, A.D., Hadly, E.A., Bascompte, J., Berlow, E.L., Brown, J.H., Fortelius, M., Getz, W.M., Harte, J., Hastings, A., Marquet, P.A., Martinez, N.D., Mooers, A., Roopnarine, P., Vermeij, G., Williams, J.W., Gillespie, R., Kitzes, J., Marshall, C., Matzke, N., Mindell, D.P., Revilla, E., & Smith, A.B. (2012). Approaching a state-shift in the Earth's biosphere. *Nature*, 486, 52–58.

Baskin, J. (2015). Paradigm dressed as epoch: the ideology of the Anthropocene. *Environmental Values*, 24(1), 9–29.

Bauer, A.M., & Ellis, E.C. (2018). The Anthropocene divide obscuring understanding of social-environmental change. *Current Anthropology*, 59(2), 209–227.

Bhambra, G.K. (2021). Colonial global economy: Towards a theoretical reorientation of political economy. *Review of International Political Economy*, 28(2), 307–322.

Biénabe, E., Boselie, D., Collion, M.-H., Fox, T., Rondot, P., van de Kop, P., & Vorley, B. (2007). The internationalization of food retailing: opportunities and threats for small-scale producers. In: Vorley, B., Fearne, A., Ray, D. (eds.), *Regoverning markets. a place for small-scale producers in modern agrifood chains?* (1st ed.), 3-18, Gower & IIED.

Bonnedahl, K.J., & Heikkurinen, P. (eds.) (2019). *Strongly sustainable societies: Organising human activities on a hot and full Earth.* Routledge.

Bonnedahl, K.J., Heikkurinen, P., & Paavola, J. (2022). Strongly sustainable development goals: Overcoming distances constraining responsible action. *Environmental Science & Policy*, 129, 150–158.

Brock, A., & Dunlap, A. (2018). Normalising corporate counterinsurgency: Engineering consent, managing resistance and greening destruction around the Hambach coal mine and beyond. *Political Geography*, 62, 33–47.

Chan, J., Pun, N., & Selden, M. (2013). The politics of global production: Apple, Foxconn and China's new working class. New Technology, *Work and Employment,* 28(2), 100–115.

Crutzen, P.J. (2002). Geology of mankind. *Nature*, 415, 23.

Crutzen, P.J., Stoermer, E.F. (2000). The Anthropocene. *Global Change Newsletter*, 41, 17–18.

Dunlap, A., & Brock, A. (2022). When the wolf guards the sheep. The industrial machine through green extractivism in Germany and Mexico. In: Mateer, J., Springer, S., Locret-Collet, M., Acker, M. (eds.), *Energies beyond the state anarchist political ecology and the liberation of nature.* Rowman & Littlefield.

Edwards, P.N., (2017). Knowledge infrastructures for the Anthropocene. *The Anthropocene Review*, 4(1), 34–43.

Elhacham, E., Ben-Uri, L., Grozovski, J., Bar-On, Y., & Milo, R. (2020). Global human-made mass exceeds all living biomass. *Nature*, 588, 442–444.

Fanon, F. (1961). *Les damne's de la terre.* Maspero, Paris.

Ferdinand, M., Chaillou, A., & Roblin, L. (2020). Why we need a decolonial ecology. *Revue Projet*, 375(2), 52–56.

Fine, B., & Leopold, E. (1993). *The world of consumption.* Routledge.

Fine, B., Bayliss, K., & Robertson, M. (2018). The systems of provision approach to understanding consumption. *The SAGE handbook of consumer culture*, 27–42. SAGE Publications.

Gadamer, H.G. (1975). Hermeneutics and social science. *Cultural Hermeneutics*, 2(4), 307–316.

Ghadge, A., Wurtmann, H., & Seuring, S. (2020). Managing climate change risks in global supply chains: a review and research agenda. *International Journal of Production Research*, 58(1), 44–64.

Gold, S., & Heikkurinen, P. (2013). Corporate responsibility, supply chain management and strategy: In search of new perspectives for sustainable food production. *Journal of Global Responsibility*, 4(2), 276–291.

Gudynas, E. (2019). Value, growth, development: South American lessons for a new ecopolitics. *Capitalist Nature Socialism*, 30(2), 234–243.

Hansen, G., & Stone, D. (2016). Assessing the observed impact of anthropogenic climate change. *Nature Climate Change*, 6(5), 532–537.

Haraway, D. (2015). Anthropocene, capitalocene, plantationocene, chthulucene: Making kin. *Environmental Humanities*, 6(1), 159–165.

Harvey, D. (2014). *Seventeen contradictions and the end of capitalism*. Oxford University Press.

Healy, N., Stephens, J.C., & Malin, S.A. (2019). Embodied energy injustices: Unveiling and politicizing the transboundary harms of fossil fuel extractivism and fossil fuel supply chains. *Energy Research and Social Science*, 48, 219–234.

Heikkurinen, P., Clegg, S., Pinnington, A.H., Nicolopoulou, K., & Alcaraz, J.M. (2021). Managing the Anthropocene: Relational agency and power to respect planetary boundaries. *Organization & Environment*, 34(2), 267–286.

Heikkurinen, P., Rinkinen, J., Järvensivu, T., Wilén, K., & Ruuska, T. (2016). Organising in the Anthropocene: An ontological outline for ecocentric theorising. *Journal of Cleaner Production*, 113, 705–714.

Heikkurinen, P. (ed.) (2017). *Sustainability and peaceful coexistence for the Anthropocene*. Routledge.

Heikkurinen, P. (2019). Degrowth: A metamorphosis in being. *Environment and Planning E: Nature and Space*, 2(3), 528–547.

Heikkurinen, P., Ruuska, T., Wilén, K., & Ulvila, M. (2019). The Anthropocene exit: Reconciling discursive tensions on the new geological epoch. *Ecological Economics*, 164, 106369.

Heikkurinen, P., Ruuska, T., Valtonen, A., & Rantala, O. (2020). Time and mobility after the Anthropocene. *Sustainability*, 12(12), 5159.

Heikkurinen, P., Clegg, S., Pinnington, A.H., Nicolopoulou, K., & Alcaraz, J.M. (2021). Managing the Anthropocene: Relational agency and power to respect planetary boundaries. *Organization & Environment*, 34(2), 267–286.

Herzberg, J., & Lorz, O. (2020). Sourcing from conflict regions: Policies to improve transparency in international supply chains. *Review of International Economics*, 28(2), 395–407.

Hickel, J. (2021). *Less is more: How degrowth will save the world*. Penguin Random House.

Hornborg, A. (2015). The political ecology of the Technocene: Uncovering ecologically unequal exchange in the world-system. In: Hamilton, C., Bonneuil, C., Gemenne, F. (eds.), *The Anthropocene and the global environmental crisis*, 57–69, Routledge.

Hultman, M., & Pulé, P. (2019). Ecological masculinities: a response to the manthropocene question? In: Gottzén, L., Mellström, U., Shefer, T. (eds.), *Routledge international handbook of masculinity studies*, 477–487, Routledge.

IPCC (2022). *Climate Change 2022: Impacts, adaptation and vulnerability*. Sixth Assessment Report of the Intergovernmental Panel on Climate Change. WMO & UNEP.

Kallis, G. (2018). *Degrowth*. Agenda Publishing.

Kallis, G., Paulson, S., D'Alisa, G., & Demaria, F. (2020). *The case for degrowth*. Polity Press.

Koenig, K. (2020). *The Amazon sacred headwaters: Indigenous rainforest 'territories for life' under threat*. Amazon Watch.

Küpers, W. (2020). From the Anthropocene to an 'Ecocene'—Eco-phenomenological perspectives on embodied, anthrodecentric transformations towards enlivening practices of organising sustainably. *Sustainability*, 12(9), 3633.

Kurth, T., Wübbels, G., Portafaix, A., Meyer zum Felde, A., & Zielcke, S. (2021). *The biodiversity crisis is a business crisis*. Boston Consulting Group.

LeBaron, G., & Lister, J. (2021). The hidden costs of global supply chain solutions. *Review of International Political Economy*, 29(3), 669–695.

Lee, J. (2016). Global supply chain dynamics and labour governance: Implications for social upgrading (April 1, 2016). ILO Research Paper No. 14, International Labour Office, Geneva.

Malm, A., & Hornborg, A. (2014). The geology of mankind? A critique of the Anthropocene narrative. *The Anthropocene Review*, 1, 62–69.

Mészáros, I. (2010). *Beyond capital: Towards a theory of Transition*. Monthly Review Press.

Mignolo, W. (2007). Delinking: The rhetoric of modernity, the logic of coloniality and the grammar of de-coloniality. *Cultural Studies*, 21(3), 476–488.

Mignolo, W. (2018). The conceptual triad. Modernity/coloniality/decoloniality. In: Mignolo, W., Walsh, K. (eds.), *On decoloniality: Concepts, analytics, praxis*. Duke University Press.

Mignolo, W. (2020). The logic of the in-visible: Decolonial reflections on the change of epoch. *Theory, Culture & Society*, 37(7–8), 205–218.

Mitchell, A.S., Lemon, M., & Lambrechts, W. (2020). Learning from the Anthropocene: Adaptive epistemology and complexity in strategic managerial thinking. *Sustainability*, 12, 4427.

Moore, J.W. (2014). The capitalocene. Part I: On the nature & origins of our ecological crisis. *The Journal of Peasant Studies*, 44(3), 1–38.

Moore, J.W. (2015). *Capitalism in the web of life. Ecology and the accumulation of capital*. Verso.

Nagurney, A. (2021). Optimization of supply chain networks with inclusion of labor: Applications to COVID-19 pandemic disruptions. *International Journal of Production Economics*, 235, 108080.

Newbold, T., Hudson, L.N., Hill, S.L.L., Contu, S., Lysenko, I., Senior, R.A., Börger, L., Bennett, D.J., Choimes, A., Collen, B., Day, J., De Palma, A., Díaz, S., Echeverria-Londoño, S., Edgar, M.J., Feldman, A., Garon, M., Harrison, M.L.K., Alhusseini, T., ... & Purvis, A. (2015). Global effects of land use on local terrestrial biodiversity. *Nature*, 520(7545), 45–50.

Nietzsche, F. ([1882-1887] 2001). *The gay science*. Edited by B, Williams. Cambridge University Press.

Obinna, D.N. (2021). Confronting disparities: race, ethnicity, and immigrant status as intersectional determinants in the COVID-19 era. *Health Education & Behavior*, 48(4), 397–403.

Patel, R., & Moore, J.W. (2017). *A history of the world in seven cheap things: A guide to capitalism, nature, and the future of the planet*. University of California Press.

Pescaroli, G., & Alexander, D. (2016). Critical infrastructure, panarchies and the vulnerability paths of cascading disasters. *Natural Hazards*, 82, 175–192.

Pescaroli, G., & Alexander, D. (2018). Understanding compound, interconnected, interacting, and cascading risks: a holistic framework. *Risk Analysis*, 38(11), 2245–2257.

Polanyi Levitt, K. (2014). Mercantilist origins of capitalism and its legacies: decline of the West and rise of the Rest. In: Velmeyer, H. (ed.), *Development in an era of neoliberal globalization*, 6–48, Routledge.

Pyysiäinen, J. (2021). Sociocultural affordances and enactment of agency: A transactional view. *Theory & Psychology*, 31(4), 491–512.

Quijano, A. (2000). Coloniality of power, Eurocentrism, and Latin America. *Nepantla: Views from South*, 1(3), 533–580.

Rinkinen, J., Shove, E., & Marsden, G. (2020). *Conceptualising demand: A distinctive approach to consumption and practice*. Routledge.

Rinkinen, J., Shove, E., & Smits, M. (2019). Cold chains in Hanoi and Bangkok: Changing systems of provision and practice. *Journal of Consumer Culture*, 19(3), 379–397.

Rinkinen, J., Shove, E., & Smits, M. (2021). Conceptualising urban density, energy demand and social practice. *Buildings & Cities*, 2(1), 79–91.

Robinson, W.I. (2014). *Global capitalism and the crisis of humanity*. Cambridge University Press.

Ross, M.L. (2004). What do we know about natural resources and civil war? *Journal of Peace Research*, 41(3), 337–356.

Ruuska, T. (2021). Conditions for alienation: Technological development and capital accumulation. In: Heikkurinen, P. & Ruuska, T. (eds.), *Sustainability beyond technology: Philosophy, critique, and implications for human organization*, 138–160, Oxford University Press.

Sasser, J.S., Leebaw, B., Ivey, C., Brown, B., Takeshita, C., & Nguyen, A. (2021). Commentary: Intersectional perspectives on COVID-19 exposure. *Journal of Exposure Science & Environmental Epidemiology*, 31, 401–403.

Shove, E., & Trentmann, F. (eds.) (2018). *Infrastructures in practice: the dynamics of demand in networked societies*. Routledge.

Simpson, D. (2012). Truth, perspectivism, and philosophy. *E-Logos: Electronic Journal for Philosophy*, 2, 1–16.

Simpson, M. (2018). The Anthropocene as colonial discourse. *Environment and Planning D: Society and Space*, 38(1), 53–71.

Steffen, W., Crutzen, P.J., & McNeill, J.R. (2007). The Anthropocene: Are humans now overwhelming the great forces of nature. *Ambio: A Journal of the Human Environment*, 36(8), 614–621.

Steffen, W., Broadgate, W., Deutsch, L., Gaffney, O., & Ludwig, C. (2015). The trajectory of the Anthropocene: The Great Acceleration. *The Anthropocene Review*, 2(1), 81–98.

Steffen, W., Richardson, K., Rockström, J., Cornell, S.E., Fetzer, I., Bennett, E.M., [...], & Sörlin, S., (2015). Planetary boundaries: Guiding human development on a changing planet. *Science*, 347, 1259855.

Steffen, W., Persson, Å., Deutsch, L., Zalasiewicz, J., Williams, M., Richardson, K., ...
    & Svedin, U. (2011). The Anthropocene: From global change to planetary steward-
    ship. *Ambio*, 40(7), 739–761.
Stephens, E.C., Martin, G., van Wijk, M., Timsina, J., & Snow, V. (2020). Editorial:
    Impacts of COVID-19 on agricultural and food systems worldwide and on progress
    to the sustainable development goals. *Agricultural Systems*, 183, 102873.
Swyngedouw, E., & Ernstson, E. (2018). Interrupting the anthropo-obScene:
    immuno-biopolitics and depoliticizing ontologies in the anthropocene. *Theory,
    Culture & Society*, 35(6), 1–28.
Tsing, A. (2009). Supply chains and the human condition. *Rethinking Marxism*, 21(2),
    148–176.
Ulvila, M., & Wilén, K. (2017). Engaging with the Plutocene: Moving towards
    degrowth and post-capitalistic futures. In: Heikkurinen, P. (ed.), *Sustainability and
    peaceful coexistence for the Anthropocene*, 119–139, Routledge.
Vadén, T. (2021). What does fossil energy tell us about technology? In: Heikkurinen,
    P. & Ruuska, T. (eds.), *Sustainability beyond technology: Philosophy, critique, and
    implications for human organization*, 138–160, Oxford University Press.
Van Dijk, L., & Rietveld, E. (2017). Foregrounding sociomaterial practice in our
    understanding of affordances: The skilled intentionality framework. *Frontiers in
    Psychology*, 7, 1969.
Vorley, B., Fearne, A., & Ray, D. (eds.) (2007). *Regoverning markets: A place for
    small-scale producers in modern agrifood chains?* (1st ed). Gower & IIED.
Waters, C.N., Zalasiewicz, J., Summerhayes, C., Barnosky, A.D., Poirier, C., Gałuszka,
    A., Cearreta, A., Edgeworth, M., Ellis, E., Ellis, M., Jeandel, C., Leinfelder, R.,
    McNeill, J.R., Richer, D., Steffen, W., Syvitski, J., Vidas, D., Wagreich, M.,
    Williams, M., An, Z., Grinevald, J., Odada, E., Oreskes, N., & Wolfe, A.P. (2016).
    The Anthropocene is functionally and stratigraphically distinct from the Holocene.
    Science, 351(6269), aad2622.
Watson, M., & Shove, E. (2022). How infrastructures and practices shape each other:
    Aggregation, integration and the introduction of gas central heating. *Sociological
    Research Online*, 28(2), 373–388.
Zalasiewicz, Jan, Waters, Colin N., Summerhayes, Colin P., Wolfe, Alexander P.,
    Barnosky, Anthony D., Cearreta, Alejandro, & Crutzen, Paul et al. (2017). The
    Working Group on the Anthropocene: Summary of evidence and interim recommen-
    dations. *Anthropocene*, 19, 55–60.

3. Fostering the crisis of supply chains: the institutional dimension

Christoph Scherrer

3.1 INTRODUCTION

The supply chain crisis is multifaceted. The current focus is on supply chain disruption caused by pandemics, trade wars, and hot wars. However, from an environmental and social sustainability perspective, this crisis dates further back. Multinational companies exploit differences in legislation and labor conditions in their global sourcing. Locations with lower environmental and/ or labor standards have been integrated into global supply chains. Although this integration has generally led to increased employment, it has also proven to be a heavy burden on the environment, and only a small portion of the total value added in the chain has benefited the companies and their workers in these low-standard sites. This is especially true for low-skilled workers, small farmers, and landless agricultural workers (Anner, 2020; Karatepe and Scherrer, 2021). This crisis, and the unfulfilled sustainability goals, is my starting point.

A major reason for the unequal distribution of value added is the power imbalances in supply chains. Much has been written about the power of leading corporations. Their superior resources and access to markets give them 'power over' their supplier base. This power enables them to capture most of the value created in the chain, thereby fostering unsustainable ecological and social practices at the beginning (Gereffi et al., 2005). Highlighting these superior resources certainly adds to the understanding of power relations in global supply chains. However, it sheds little light on the factors that enable and sustain these leading companies. The focus on a dyadic (i.e., business-to-business) relationship neglects the many actors that stand outside this two-way relationship but influences them, such as financial institutions, accounting firms, unions, and, of course, the state.

The literature on global production networks (Henderson et al., 2002) and production systems (Barrientos and Smith, 2007) draws attention to the other actors and the institutions that shape their identities, perceptions of interests, and behavior. The role of institutions for human behavior is the focus of sociological institutionalism. This paradigm contributes the important insight that the institutional context, such as the legal framework, is of great importance for the possibility of exercising power among actors (Eckardt and Poletti, 2018).

The aim of my contribution is therefore to shed light on the institutional context of global supply chains and to show how this context contributes to the overwhelming power of the leading companies and thus to the social sustainability crisis of the chains. My analysis of the institutional context will be guided by the distinction between regulative, normative, and cognitive institutions in sociological institutionalism. I illustrate the theoretical arguments mainly with reference to smallholder farms. Agriculture still employs nearly one-third of the world's workforce. The decent work deficit is comparatively more pronounced in agriculture (Scherrer and Verma, 2018).

3.2   INSTITUTIONS AS FOUNDATIONS OF THE EXERCISE OF POWER

A sociological perspective on markets emphasizes their embeddedness in broader economic, political, and social institutions. These institutions shape the interests, worldviews, and behavior of market participants, be they producers, brokers, or consumers (Olds and Thrift, 2005).

There is a plethora of definitions of institutions. I define them as patterns of human meaning-making and practices (Eckhardt and Poletti, 2018). The origins of these patterns are diverse; they range from dictatorially imposed and enforced rules to the spontaneous, decentralized diffusion of ideas or practices. The distinction between regulative, normative, and cognitive institutions in sociological institutionalism (Meyer and Rowan, 1977; DiMaggio and Powell, 1983; Scott, 2001) provides an analytical framework for understanding the institutional aspects of power relations in global supply chains. Regulative institutions include institutionalized understandings of government policies and bureaucratic requirements; normative institutions are values and norms; and cognitive institutions include systems of meaning-making (see Munir, 2002).

3.2.1   Regulatory Institutions

Regulatory institutions are laws and regulations enacted, interpreted, and adjudicated by governments (including supranational and international organizations), regulatory agencies, and courts (see Bello et al., 2004).

Laws as regulative institutions form the basis for authoritative power and its legitimate exercise of power. Decisive for the exercise of power in companies are national constitutions that establish the inviolability of private property.

These constitutions give owners the power to dispose of their property; therefore, the owners' decisions acquire an authoritative character and appear legitimate. Of course, constitutional law also imposes certain limitations on owners' discretionary powers, which are further restricted by national laws, especially corporate and labor laws. Of great importance to focal companies in global supply chains is their status as legal entities, which had to be fought for over a long period of time (Pistor, 2019). This status allows them to contract with other firms and individuals and to use courts to enforce their contractual rights (Bello et al., 2004).

Over time, property rights have been extended to include ownership of intellectual achievements such as inventions of products, processes, and software (patents), of names (trademarks) and of production areas (geographical indications). Patents, trademarks, and geographical indications protect the 'first movers', the technological pioneers, from imitators. The first movers have traditionally been based in the formal colonial powers; only in recent years, some other countries, notably the People's Republic of China, have been applying for patents and trademarks on a large scale (Statista, 2019). Patents support the power of the focal firm, especially in producer-driven chains; they limit market entry.

Brand names underpin branding strategies, especially in buyer-driven chains, with the consequence of limiting access to end consumers. Geographical indications, such as Champagne or Parma cheese (Belletti et al., 2017), also favor 'Old World' agricultural producers over newcomers, as they have had more time to build a reputation for good products among prestigious consumers who tend to have more money.

An example of the difficulties faced by producers from the Global South in marketing their products internationally can be found in the 'old' Punjab, which comprises today's Pakistani and Indian Punjab and Indian Haryana, the traditional growing region of basmati rice. Rice producers there had to defend themselves against patent claims by a Texas producer. Pakistani and Indian basmati growers have only recently been granted geographical indication status, which is still controversial in India. In contrast, coffee growers are not in direct competition with northern producers. But their attempts to market either their territory or their specific coffee variety require great collective effort and are not always crowned with success. With a few exceptions, such as Juan Valdez Café and Cerrado Coffee, the brands of international roasters and coffee house chains dominate the market (Karatepe and Scherrer, 2021).

The powers of intellectual property rights holders in global supply chains are strengthened by international treaties. The 'Agreement on Trade-Related Aspects of Intellectual Property Rights' (TRIPS) concluded in 1995 within the framework of the World Trade Organization (WTO) and the multiplying preferential trade agreements between different countries allow not only the seizure of goods that are proven to infringe intellectual property rights (TRIPS Part III), but also trade sanctions against the state that is not willing to comply with the agreement (TRIPS Part V; see Panagariya, 2004).

3.2.1.1 World trade rules

The effect of protecting property rights is not exhausted by pointing to pioneers and imitators. Property rights in the means of production promote competition. Most scholars rightly identify competition as a central constraint for members of a production network (Coe and Yeung, 2019). However, it also provides power opportunities, especially for focal firms. On the one hand, competition among focal firms forces them to become increasingly innovative and/or cost-efficient, hence, weaker firms are ousted, leading to higher market concentration (Kumar, 2020). On the other hand, competition provides them with a 'pretext' to demand concessions from their suppliers and employees based on the credible threat that it poses to the entire network (Bronfenbrenner, 2000). Of course, other firms in the network may also support demands for more favorable contract terms from their business partners (and wage earners) who are more dependent on them than vice versa.

The two fundamental principles of the world trade regime administered by the WTO protect foreign companies from being discriminated against vis-à-vis domestic competitors. The most-favored-nation (MFN) principle requires a country to grant any concessions, privileges, or immunities granted to one nation in a trade agreement to other WTO members as well. The principle of national treatment prohibits discrimination between imported and domestically produced goods or services with respect to government regulations (see the WTO's website). For example, health regulations may not be more stringent for imported food than for domestic food. Together with the ubiquitous investment treaties that protect foreign investors (UNCTAD, 2019), these principles are essential to the functioning of transnational corporations and global sourcing.

Moreover, thanks to their subsidiaries abroad, transnational corporations are particularly well positioned to take advantage of the WTO dispute settlement process by lobbying both the domestic government and the host government involved in a dispute about violations of WTO rules (Yildirim et al., 2018). For example, in 2019, Guatemala accused India of non-WTO compatible domestic support measures for its sugarcane production in a WTO dispute (WTO, n.d.). Guatemala's sugarcane milling industry is dominated by the transnational corporation Pantaleon and their politically well-connected owners (Alonso-Fradejas, 2018). The same is true of the so-called investor-state dispute settlement proceedings (Kahale, 2018). For example, the US transnational corporation Bechtel used the bilateral investment treaty between India and Mauritius to obtain compensation of 160 million US dollars for the decision of the government of the Indian state of Maharashtra to cancel the Dabhol project, a gas-fired electricity plant. As the project had threatened the livelihood of the surrounding fishing communities, these communities had successfully protested against its completion (UNCTAD, n.d.).

At the national level, for example, the establishment of 'export-processing zones' has often been used to reduce labor protection (McCallum, 2011). Their main purpose is to free the flow of parts within a cross-border supply chain from customs hurdles.

3.2.1.2 International tax regime

The question of how to increase the share of value added occupies a prominent place in the value-added literature. The secondary distributional effects, however, are usually overlooked. David Quentin and Liam Campling (2018) have pointed to the tax avoidance strategies of focal firms. The institution of international tax sovereignty (i.e., the freedom of countries to set their tax rates), together with the deliberate absence of an international tax regime, allow transnational corporations to declare profits in so-called tax havens rather than where the value creation took place. For example, the world's largest grain traders ADM, Bunge, Cargill and Dreyfus have been accused of massive tax evasion by the Argentine government (Lawrence, 2011).

For my concern here, namely, to shed light on the phenomenon of power, this lack of a coordinated international tax regime is not least a consequence of the power of transnational corporations (Palan et al., 2010). At the same time, it increases the power of these corporations by providing them with additional quantities of a key resource, namely, money. The extra money can be used to strengthen the position of the tax-avoiding corporation by acquiring other firms and investing in research and development, marketing, logistics, lobbying, and so on.

In addition, institutionally enabled tax avoidance affects the state capacity of host countries. As can be learned from the strand in the global production networks literature on economic upgrading strategies well-designed state policies can help local firms move up the value chain (Herr, 2019; Rodrik, 2004). These policies, which include investments in education, infrastructure, and industry clusters, for example, are compromised when the host state does not receive sufficient revenue through tax avoidance (e.g., Bangladesh; Anner and Hossain, 2016). The tax avoidance regime leads to what Leonard Seabrooke and Duncan Wigan (2014) call global wealth chains, which reinforce inequality.

3.2.1.3 Financial regime

The liberal international financial regime, with easy cross-border financial transactions, contributes to the power of focal corporations. Money is the most fungible resource: It can be used in many ways, as mentioned earlier. The speed with which it can be mobilized can be critical to competitive advantage. Because of their power position in the supply chain, focal firms command usually over the largest financial resources. Therefore, a liberal financial regime enhances their power. Investment in advanced technologies gives them efficiency gains, and the acquisition of smaller competitors increases their market share and thus their bargaining power. This has led to further market concentration. Grocery chains and farm input suppliers are also increasingly involved in financial activities; for example, Wal-Mart and Tesco offer their customers an increasingly wide range of financial products, including credit and prepaid credit cards, savings and checking accounts, insurance programs, and even mortgages (Clapp and Isakson, 2018).

However, focal companies are not the only ones to benefit from the processes of 'financialization' that give rise to institutions such as a 'market for corporate control'. The vast liquid sums available to banks, institutional investors, and hedge funds enable them to buy or threaten to buy even the largest companies, thereby taking control or influencing corporate decisions, even to the point of selling large parts of those companies (Höpner and Jackson, 2006). Thus, financial actors are potentially the most powerful in global production networks. Like the competitive effect described above, the threat of a takeover by financial actors can be used by the top management to limit the value creation of the company's stakeholders, such as employees, as well as suppliers. To fend off hostile takeovers, a company's stock market value must increase, which can most easily be achieved through profit increases and/or share buybacks. However, the disproportionate increases in executive salaries show that not only shareholders but also top management benefit from this strategy (Lazonick, 2016).

3.2.1.4 Human rights

So far, I have focused on regulatory institutions that enable and reinforce the exercise of power by strong members in global production systems. Institutions that potentially support the weak should not be left out. At the international level, the United Nations International Covenant on Civil and Political Rights and the International Covenant on Economic, Social and Cultural Rights, as well as the labor rights and standards conventions of the International Labor Organization (ILO), define a broad range of rights for people living in the member countries of these international organizations. With few exceptions, the granting and enforcement of these rights rests with the individual state. One exception is the European Court of Human Rights (ECHR). It acts as an appellate body for citizens whose rights have been denied by their respective national courts in the current 47 European member states. The opportunities for individual petitioners to be heard at the international level are generally very limited (Dantas, 2012). No international agreement or convention covers the rights of small versus large companies.

National legal protection of smallholder farms varies widely from country to country; in some countries, they do not even enjoy secure rights over their land (Deiniger, 2013). Labor laws also vary from country to country. In quite a few countries, farm workers are not covered by labor laws (ILO, 2019). However, most countries are signatories to core ILO conventions that require countries to uphold certain rights of wage earners. While the ILO's founding in 1919 was driven primarily by concern for factory workers, the organization adopted the 'Right to Organize (Agriculture) Convention (No. 11)' as early as 1921. Since then, it has enacted over 30 international labor standards specific to agriculture. However, few countries have ratified these conventions, with the exception of No. 11, reflecting on the general political neglect of agricultural labor. While enforcement of these rights relies almost exclusively on the weak tool of 'naming and shaming', labor rights norms in international law confer legitimacy on those who demand actual protection of these rights (Koliev and Lebovic, 2018).

At the national level, the degree of access to justice, the speed of court proceedings, and the impartiality of judges appear to be the key determinants of the extent to which regulatory institutions support the rights (ICCE, 2018) and thus the bargaining power of wage earners, farmers, and small businesses. In other words, the potential of regulatory institutions to support the weak members of production systems needs to be interrogated at the relevant national and sometimes regional level. For example, the lack of speedy trials for poor people in India is well documented (Galanter and Krishnan, 2003). Overall, then, people in agriculture who are involved in global production systems are afforded less legal protection than those in the industry.

3.2.2 Normative Institutions

Group values and norms represent normative institutions that guide human behavior through social obligations and expectations (Scott, 2001). In today's business world, the most important social obligation is compliance with the relevant law. However, it is also accepted that business people try to interpret the law in their favor or find loopholes that exempt them from the law (e.g., banking regulation; van Staveren 2020). The social norms that shape organizational cultures can influence behavior more than laws (Ellickson, 1998). The widely held expectation of business people's behavior is that they seek profit. The extent to which the pursuit of profit takes precedence over other goals, such as concern for the welfare of the community, is context-specific.

The increasing call for corporate social responsibility has led many focal companies to establish corresponding departments and to include social goals in their published mission statements. However, these concerns are not 'mainstreamed' in most focal companies (Schneider, 2019). The routines of most purchasing and sales departments follow the age-old dictum of 'buy cheap and sell dear'. These routines have their own legitimacy, namely, the weight of habit and their proven functionality. Moreover, they are supported by appropriate incentive systems and reinforced by the aforementioned competition among companies. The constant demands of the purchasing departments of international clothing companies for price reductions at their supplier factories are well documented (see Anner, 2020). The attempt by the supermarket chain Lidl to offer a better price to banana plantations in South America in the spirit of social sustainability failed due to competition that significantly undercut banana prices in Lidl's stores.[1] In other words, these business routines are relatively inert, resistant to change.

In companies, those who work for the company are expected to follow the orders of those who are above them in the hierarchy. Again, the extent to which orders must be followed and disagreement is accepted is context-specific (Ortmann, 2010). The specific contexts are influenced not only by the regulatory institutions mentioned earlier (e.g., labor law), but also by norms of fairness and traditions of contestation. What is considered fair varies from country to country, and in some cases from place to place. Wage levels alone show huge differences: $18 per day for harvesters on Brazilian coffee plantations versus $3 in India (Chi et al., 2021). And, where trade unions or other collective representations have been established, management orders are met differently than in companies without such representations or positive experience of industrial action.

3.2.3   Cognitive Institutions

Cognitive institutions provide individuals and groups with a framework for making meaning of events and environments. They guide actors' behavior with 'prefabricated organizing models and scripts' (Scott, 2001, p. 58). While normative institutions prescribe socially acceptable behavior, 'cognitive institutions lead to 'reflex' action, which is deeply ingrained in individuals and difficult to transcend' (Munir, 2002, p. 1412).

Applied to the question of power in global production systems, a cognitive framework widely used in the business world comes to mind: technical rationality. The focus on efficiently achieving a particular purpose (i.e., increasing revenue and reducing costs) leaves less room for goals that do not easily fall under the dictates of efficiency, such as giving all stakeholders a voice or supporting the economic upgrading of a supplier. Technical rationality usually favors the interests of the top management at various points in the chain (cf. Fleming and Spicer, 2007).

Technically efficient practices spread through a process called 'cognitive isomorphism' (Meyer and Rowan, 1977). Companies copy these practices from one another, with the diffusion of certain practices accelerated by consulting firms, business schools, business journals, and professional associations. The practices that are disseminated may not be the most effective for the adopting company, but because they are generally considered the most appropriate, their implementation is accepted as legitimate (Fleming and Spicer, 2007). Those who implement them are likely to face less resistance in doing so. The so-called Green Revolution is a good example of the discursive power of technical efficiency, as demonstrated by the recent critical assessments of the Alliance for a Green Revolution in Africa (Wise, 2020), funded by the Bill and Melinda Gates Foundation. This serves the purpose of promoting agricultural mechanization and advancing seed hybridization and the use of chemical fertilizers and pesticides.

Technical rationality in the form of simple heuristics (i.e., making decisions with limited knowledge and little time; Gigerenzer et al., 1999), may also favor the persistence of prejudices. The management of focal companies may have prejudices against certain types of companies, companies from certain locations, or certain ethnic or educational backgrounds of employees (cf. Fligstein, 1987). This may lead either to systematic exclusion of these enterprises or wage earners or to justifications for imposing particularly onerous contract terms on them. In Vietnam, for example, minority-owned coffee plantations receive less agronomic support and are less likely to be included in cooperatives that provide health insurance for their members, among other benefits (Chi et al., 2021).

From the suppliers' perspective, harsh contractual conditions can also be something normal and thus acceptable if steep hierarchies were part of their lives. This is especially true for farmers who still live in semi-feudal communities, as is still partly the case in India (Bhowmik, 2009).

Cognitive isomorphism may not only work in favor of current exploitative practices, but it is conceivable that stakeholder practices will also gain more legitimacy through demonstrated sustainability and a growing literature on social and environmental management.

3.3   CONCLUSION

As much as global procurement involves a multitude of actors who do not fit into a metaphorical chain, the relationship between two actors is embedded in a complex web of institutions. Sociological institutionalism draws our attention to regulative, normative, and cognitive institutions that shape interactions within global production systems. The ability of transnational corporations to source globally rests on their legal status as legal entities, intellectual property rights enforced through international treaties, and trade agreements that protect them from discrimination against local competitors. A liberal financial regime that ensures the free flow of money across borders, along with a variety of bilateral investment treaties, allows the wealthy to capture a disproportionate share of value creation in production systems.

A central social obligation in contemporary societies is compliance with the law. However, this norm clashes with the widespread role expectation of businesspeople as profit maximizers. Interpreting a law in one's own favor and looking for loopholes is an accepted practice. The strength of this competing norm to law-abiding behavior is reflected in the comparatively low punishment when a court has found a law to have been violated. The result is large-scale tax avoidance and evasion, as well as the violation of human rights. Among cognitive institutions, technical rationality plays an important role in global production systems. This widely shared cognitive framework leaves little room for goals beyond narrow efficiency dictates, such as stakeholder concerns.

Because of the interconnectedness of these key institutions, attempts to address power imbalances by changing a particular institution are likely to fail. Corporate social responsibility or fair-trade initiatives address far too narrow a segment of this institutional configuration to achieve their stated goals. Their function, usually unintentional, is ultimately to prevent fundamental criticism of current business practices. Therefore, to overcome the long-simmering social crisis in supply chains, a comprehensive questioning of a broad range of institutions is needed.

NOTE

1. See www.lebensmittelpraxis.de/ sortiment/ 24139 -bananen -preis -der -fairness .html (9/28/2021).

REFERENCES

Alonso-Fradejas, A. (2018). The Rise of Agro-Extractive Capitalism. Insights from Guatemala in the Early 21st Century. International Institute of Social Studies, Erasmus University Rotterdam.

Anner, M. (2020). Squeezing Workers' Rights in Global Supply Chains: Purchasing Practices in the Bangladesh Garment Export Sector in Comparative Perspective. *Review of International Political Economy*, 27(2), 320–347.

Anner, M., & Hossain, J. (2016). Multinational Corporations and Economic Inequality in the Global South. In: Gallas, A. et al. (eds.), *Combating Inequality*, 93–110, Routledge.

Barrientos, S., & Smith, S. (2007). Do Workers Benefit from Ethical Trade? Assessing Codes of Labour Practice in Global Production Systems. *Third World Quarterly*, 28(4), 713–729.

Belletti, G., Marescotti, A., & Touzard, J.-M. (2017). Geographical Indications, Public Goods, and Sustainable Development: The Roles of Actors' Strategies and Public Policies. *World Development*, 98, 45–57.

Bello, D.C., Lohtia, R., & Sangtani, V. (2004). An Institutional Analysis of Supply Chain Innovations in Global Marketing Channels. *Industrial Marketing Management*, 33, 57–64.

Bhowmik, S.K. (2009). Unfree Labour in the Plantation System. In: Breman, J., Guérin, I., Prakash, A. (eds.), *India's Unfree Workforce: Of Bondage Old and New*, 312–333, Oxford University Press.

Bronfenbrenner, K. (2000). Raw Power: Plant-Closing Threats and the Threat to Union Organizing. *Multinational Monitor*, 21(12), 24–29.

Chi, D.Q., Hawkins, D., de Jesus, C.M., Ortega, A.C., Perosa, B.B., Verma, S., Karatepe, I.D., & Scherrer, C. (2021). Economic and Social Upgrading in the Coffee VC in a Comparative Perspective. In: Karatepe, I.D., & Scherrer, C. (eds.). *The Phantom of Upgrading in Agricultural Supply Chains: A Cross-Country, Cross-Crop Comparison of Smallholders*, 111–173, Nomos.

Clapp, J., & Isakson, S.R. (2018). *Speculative Harvests: Financialization, Food, and Agriculture*. Practical Action Publishing.

Coe, N.M., & Yeung, H.W.-C. (2019). Global Production Networks: Mapping Recent Conceptual Developments. *Journal of Economic Geography*, 19(4), 775–801.

Dantas, C. (2012). Right of Petition by Individuals within the Global Human Rights Protection System. *SUR - International Journal on Human Rights*, 9(17), 187–207.

Deiniger, K. (2013). Securing Land Rights for Smallholder Farmers. In: Hazell, P.B.R., & Atiqur, R. (eds.), *New Directions for Smallholder Agriculture*, 401–433, Oxford University Press.

DiMaggio, P.J., & Powell, W.W. (1983). The Iron Cage Revisited: Institutional Isomorphism and Collective Rationality in Organizational Fields. *American Sociological Review*, 48, 147–160.

Eckhardt, J., & Poletti, A. (2018). Introduction: Bringing Institutions Back in the Study of Global Value Chains. *Global Policy*, 9, 5–11.

Ellickson, R.C. (1998). Law and Economics Discovers Social Norms. *Journal of Legal Studies*, 27(2), 537–552.

Fleming, P., & Spicer, A. (2007). *Contesting the Corporation*. Cambridge University Press.

Fligstein, N. (1987). The Intraorganizational Power Struggle: Rise of Finance Personnel to Top Leadership in Large Corporations, 1919–1979. *American Sociological Review*, 52(1), 44–58.

Galanter, M., & Krishnan, J.K. (2003). Bread for the Poor: Access to Justice and the Rights of the Needy in India. *Hastings Law Journal*, 55(4), 789–834.

Gereffi, G., Humphrey, J., & Sturgeon, T. (2005). The Governance of Global Value Chains. *Review of International Political Economy*, 12(1), 78–104.

Gigerenzer, G., Todd, P.M., & ABC Research Group (1999). *Simple Heuristics That Make Us Smart*. Oxford University Press.

Henderson, J., Dicken, P., Hess, M., Coe, N., & Yeung, H. (2002). Global Production Networks and the Analysis of Economic Development. *Review of International Political Economy*, 9(3), 436–464.

Herr, H. (2019). *Industrial Policy for Economic and Social Upgrading in Developing Countries*. Friedrich-Ebert-Foundation (ed.), Singapur.

Höpner, M., & Jackson, G. (2006). Revisiting the Mannesmann Takeover: How Markets for Corporate Control Emerge. *European Management Review*, 3, 142–155.

ICCE - International Consortium for Court Excellence (2018). Global Measures of Court Performance. Melbourne. https://www.courtexcellence.com

International Labour Office (ILO) (2019). Decent and Productive Work in Agriculture: Decent Work in the Rural Economy, Policy Guidance Notes. https://www.ilo.org/wcmsp5/groups/public/---ed_dialogue/---sector/documents/publication/wcms_437173.pdf

Kahale III, G. (2018). The Inaugural Brooklyn Lecture on International Business Law: »ISDS: The Wild, Wild West of International Practice«. *Brooklyn Journal of International Law*, 44(1).

Karatepe, I.D., & Scherrer, C. (eds.) (2021). *The Phantom of Upgrading in Agricultural Supply Chains. A Cross-Country, Cross-Crop Comparison of Smallholders*. Nomos.

Koliev, F., & Lebovic, J.H. (2018). Selecting for Shame: The Monitoring of Workers' Rights by the International Labour Organization, 1989 to 2011. *International Studies Quarterly*, 62(2), 437–452.

Kumar, A. (2020). *Monopsony Capitalism: Power and Production in the Twilight of the Sweatshop Age*. Cambridge University Press.

Lawrence, F. (2011). Argentina Accuses World's Largest Grain Traders of Huge Tax Evasion. *The Guardian*, 1 June. https://www.theguardian.com/business/2011/jun/01/argentina-accuses-grain-traders-tax-evasion

Lazonick, W. (2016). The Value-Extracting CEO: How Executive Stock-Based Pay Undermines Investment in Productive Capabilities. Institute for New Economic Thinking (ed.), Working Paper 54.

McCallum, J.K. (2011). Export processing zones. Comparative data from China, Honduras, Nicaragua and South Africa. Working paper 21. Industrial and Employment Relations Department, International Labour Office, Geneva.

Meyer, J.W., & Rowan, B. (1977). Institutionalized Organizations: Formal Structure as Myth and Ceremony. *American Journal of Sociology*, 83(2), 340–363.

Munir, K.A. (2002). Being Different: How Normative and Cognitive Aspects of Institutional Environments Influence Technology Transfer. *Human Relations*, 55(12), 1403–1428.

Olds, K., & Thrift, N. (2005). Cultures on the Brink: Reengineering the Soul of Capitalism on a Global Scale. In: Ong, A., & Collier, S.J. (eds.), *Global assemblages: Technology, politics, and ethics as anthropological problems*, 270–290, Blackwell Publishing.

Ortmann, G. (2010). On Drifting Rules and Standards. *Scandinavian Journal of Management*, 26(2), 204–214.

Palan, R., Murphy, R., & Chavagneux, C. (2010). *Tax Havens: How Globalization Really Works*. Cornell University Press.

Panagariya, A. (2004). TRIPs and the WTO: An Uneasy Marriage. In: Maskus, K. (ed.), *The WTO, Intellectual Property Rights and the Knowledge Economy*. Edward Elgar Publishing.

Pistor, K. (2019). *The Code of Capital*. Princeton University Press.

Quentin, D., & Campling, L. (2018). Global Inequality Chains: Integrating Mechanisms of Value Distribution into Analyses of Global Production. *Global Networks*, 18, 33–56.

Rodrik, D. (2004). *Industrial Policy for the Twenty-First Century*. John F. Kennedy School of Government.

Scherrer, C., & Verma, S. (eds.) (2018). *Decent Work Deficits in Southern Agriculture: Measurements, Drivers and Strategies*. Rainer Hampp Verlag.

Schneider, A. (2019). Bound to Fail? Exploring the Systemic Pathologies of CSR and Their Implications for CSR Research. *Business & Society*, 59(22), 1303–1338.

Scott, W.R. (2001). *Institutions and Organizations*. Sage.

Seabrooke, L., & Wigan, D. (2014). Global Wealth Chains in the International Political Economy. *Review of International Political Economy*, 21(1), 257–263.

Statista (2019). Ranking of the 20 National Patent Offices with the Most Patent Applications in 2019. http:// statista .com/ statistics/ 257114/ ranking -of -the -20 -countries-with-the-most-patent-applications/

UNCTAD (2019). Taking Stock of IIA Reform: Recent Developments. IIAs Issue Note #3.

UNCTAD (no date). Bechtel vs. India. https://investmentpolicy.unctad.org/investment -dispute-settlement/cases/104/bechtel-v-india

van Staveren, I. (2020). The Misdirection of Bankers' Moral Compass in the Organizational Field of Banking. *Cambridge Journal of Economics*, 44, 507–526.

Wise, T.A. (2020). Failing Africa's Farmers: An Impact Assessment of the Alliance for a Green Revolution in Africa. Global Development and Environment Institute, Working Paper 20-01, Medford.

WTO (n.d.). Dispute Settlement DS581: India – Measures Concerning Sugar and Sugarcane. https://www.wto.org/english/tratop_e/dispu_e/cases_e/ds581_e.htm

Yildirim, A.B., Tyson Chatagnier, J., Poletti, A., & De Bièvre, D. (2018). The Internationalization of Production and the Politics of Compliance in WTO Disputes. *The Review of International Organizations*, 13, 49–75.

PART II

Symptoms of the crisis

4. The global regulation of supply chains and human rights: linked but fractured

Janne Mende

4.1   INTRODUCTION

Supply chains' relevance for national and global economies, trade, employees, consumers and other stakeholders has increased tremendously in recent decades, accompanied by the promise to contribute to economic prosperity. At the same time, doubts over their positive effects have risen, diagnosing their crisis by juxtaposing that promise with harsh reality (cf. Chapter 1: The supply chain in crisis, this volume). One of these harsh realities concerns the effect of supply chains on human rights. On the one hand, human rights concerns are somewhat overshadowed by the economic effects of supply chains—and their interruptions, as vividly demonstrated during the Covid-19 pandemic, or the Russian offensive war in Ukraine. On the other hand, the effects of supply chains on human rights are remarkably visible, including, for instance, the risk of famine as a result of the interruption of Ukrainian grain exports, or the undue working conditions among suppliers for global companies in the textile sector. Thus, one might think that by now the relation between the global regulation of supply chains and human rights is being given full consideration. However, the picture is more complex than that, and the relation continues to be ambiguous.

This chapter explores this ambiguous relation between the global regulation of supply chains and human rights, and investigates the reasons for it. It conducts an in-depth analysis of current discussions in the issue area of business and human rights, namely the United Nations (UN) treaty process, which aims at an international regulation of business conduct with regard to human rights. This process partly interconnects supply chain regulation with human rights, yet demonstrates the cracks in their relationship. Both the output side (in the form of draft treaties) and input side (in the form of stakeholder comments) of the process show that while supply chains represent only a small part of the deliberations—and even disappear from the draft treaties' language—their relevance, measures and challenges have strong (yet fractured) links to the regulation of business activities with regard to human rights. This analysis helps discuss the potential of, as well as the challenges posed by, the three regulatory dimensions of business power, the bindingness of regulation, and the policy level of regulation. Thus, better understanding this linked but fractured relationship builds a basis for further developing the regulation of supply chains from a human rights perspective.

In this chapter, Section 2 introduces the relation between supply chains and human rights, and provides a short overview of the institutional separation between labor rights and human rights. Section 3 studies the UN treaty process and how it links supply chains and their regulation to human rights. Section 4 discusses the regulatory potential of their linked but fractured relationship, followed by a brief conclusion.

4.2   SUPPLY CHAINS AND HUMAN RIGHTS

As this chapter focuses on the global and international regulation of supply chains in their different forms, it draws on a broad definition of supply chains as denoting 'borderless production systems—which may be sequential chains or complex networks and which may be global, regional or span only two countries' (UNCTAD, 2013, p. 122).[1] This includes downstream (consumer), as well as upstream (supplier) relationships in the Global North and South, and consists of both formal and informal ties. The concepts of global networks or global production systems involve different policy levels, actors and institutions, and emphasize—alongside formal chains of control and subsidiaries— the role of loose networks with all kinds of suppliers without legal ownership (Barrientos et al., 2011). While some definitions of supply chains include such loose networks, others criticize the term 'supply chains' for its inability to take such broader business relationships and further actors such as investors into account. This ambivalence reappears in the human rights discussions below, with measures directed at subsidiaries accompanied by efforts to address other actors as well. Accordingly, it also marks the regulatory potential and limits of supply chain regulation, as discussed below.

4.2.1   Supply Chains' Relevance for Human Rights

In 2013, global supply chains accounted for 60% of global trade (UNCTAD, 2013). While their relative importance has gradually stagnated since 2010, participation in supply chains continues to rise in absolute terms (UNCTAD, 2018). The ILO estimates that approximately 450 million workers were involved in global supply chains as of 2013.[2] Given the importance of supply chains for economics, state politics, companies, and working conditions, their impact on human rights seems evident. A vital body of research addresses how human rights regulation can (or cannot) affect supply chain dynamics, and vice versa (Arnold and Bowie, 2007; Locke et al. 2009; Pagnattaro 2014; Clarke and Boersma, 2017). This concerns labor rights in particular (Fenwick and Novitz, 2010; Mantouvalou, 2012; Saner and Yiu, 2020). In addition, supply chains are relevant for human rights beyond the workplace, such as when companies and suppliers fuel land grabbing and deprivation of food, housing and other basic needs, or when they cause or facilitate environmental damage, political oppression and restrictions on humanitarian rights (Wettstein, 2009; Morrison, 2011).

These issues have particularly come to the fore in the issue area of business and human rights (BHR), which focuses on the regulation of companies with regard to human rights. The BHR discourse gained momentum in the 1990s, when civil society organizations began to target Western-based transnational companies for their human rights violations in the Global South (Avery, 2000), and international lawyers started to address the role of non-state actors in the traditionally state-centered international human rights regime (Clapham, 1993; Alston, 2005; Andreopoulos et al., 2006). BHR regulation was massively fueled by the endorsement of the United Nations Guiding Principles on Business and Human Rights (UNGPs) in 2011. These provide the major reference point for further developments and criticism, particularly regarding the appropriate mix of non-binding responsibilities and self-regulation of companies on the one hand, and greater accountability for human rights and binding regulations on the other (Ramasastry, 2015), currently culminating in the UN treaty process.

4.2.2   The International Regulation of Human Rights and Labor Rights

One reason for the ambiguous relation between the regulation of supply chains and human rights lies in the organization of international relations and its segmentation of international law (e.g., trade law, environmental law, cf. Krisch, 2021). Accordingly, international treaties and agreements treat labor rights and human rights separately, which is visible in their differentiated institutionalization within the International Labour Organization (ILO) and the UN.

On the one hand, the ILO addresses supply chains mainly in terms of their impact on labor rights and labor conditions—including decent working conditions, social protection, bargaining and association rights, child labor, forced labor, slavery and the protection of women and minorities (Gold et al., 2015; Crane et al., 2017; Scherrer, 2017). The ILO was founded in 1919, decades before the international human rights regime was established with the founding of the UN in 1945.[3]

The concept of human rights (among others shaped and developed in the UN), on the other hand, encompasses a highly diverse range of issue areas; supply chains are just one part. Furthermore, for a long time, UN debates on human rights focused on civil and political rights rather than social rights, which often include labor rights. This separation is manifested in the two core human rights treaties—the International Covenant on Civil and Political Rights and the International Covenant on Economic, Social and Cultural Rights. Their diverging developments, monitoring and implementation mechanisms caused a neglect of social and economic rights that has only recently been caught up (Craven, 1998; Schutter et al. 2012).

The ILO labor rights regime also differs from the UN human rights regime with regard to its outcome: the ILO's standards lend themselves to a more detailed and technical regulation than the more fundamental UN human rights (Ebert, n.d.). At the same time, this difference may enable productive cross-regulation (Servais and van Goethem, 2016). The ILO and UN also have different participation structures. While the ILO's tripartism includes worker and employer associations in its deliberations, decision-making processes and standards (Ebert, n.d.), UN human rights fora focus on individuals, and non-state actors such as unions have only recently been partially included (Steffek and Hahn, 2010).

The separate institutionalization of labor rights and human rights, however, provides only a partial explanation for the ambiguous relation between the regulation of supply chains and human rights—not least because supply chains affect human rights other than labor rights as well. In order to explain this further, the remainder of this paper provides an in-depth study of the UN treaty process.

4.3   THE UN TREATY PROCESS ON BUSINESS AND HUMAN RIGHTS

The UN treaty process represents one of the most current and controversial discussions on regulating businesses with regard to human rights on a global level. It is represented by the open-ended intergovernmental working group (IGWG) on transnational corporations and other business enterprises with respect to human rights, initiated by the UN Human Rights Council in 2014. With a mandate to 'elaborate an international legally binding instrument to regulate, in international human rights law, the activities of transnational corporations and other business enterprises' (UN Doc. A/HRC/RES/26/9), the IGWG has convened annual meetings since 2015 and is developing drafts for a future treaty.

Supply chains play an ambiguous role in the treaty process. On the one hand, the term 'supply chains' disappears from the treaty language, as the following overview of the treaty process's output side demonstrates (Section 3.1). However, the relevance of and the measures and challenges related to supply chain regulation (SCR) represent strong links to human rights regulation in the treaty process's input side. Sections 3.2 to 3.4 elaborate these links and their fractures in depth, based on a qualitative analysis of the treaty process that assesses the commentaries and statements made by all stakeholders directly or indirectly involved in it. The analysis spans from the Human Rights Council's discussion about whether to initiate the working group in 2013 to the latest comments on the first draft treaty in December 2018. The sample includes nearly 1,000 documents (Mende, 2020a) that have been submitted to the IGWG or published as a commentary on its work.[4]

4.3.1   Supply Chains in the Draft Treaties

In 2018, after three annual meetings characterized by broad and controversial discussions, the IGWG published its first draft treaty, the so-called Zero Draft, which addressed supply chains in Article 10.6:

> All persons with business activities of a transnational character shall be liable for harm caused by violations of human rights arising in the context of their business activities, including throughout their operations:
> a.   to the extent it exercises control over the operations, or
> b.   to the extent it exhibits a sufficiently close relation with its subsidiary or entity in its supply chain and where there is strong and direct connection between its conduct and the wrong suffered by the victim, or
> c.   to the extent risk have been foreseen or should have been foreseen of human rights violations within its chain of economic activity.

However, the terms 'supply chains' or 'value chains' disappeared from the First Revised Draft in 2019, which subsumed the matter under the broader formulation of contractual relationships and control. This change provoked the following criticism:

> it is not clear how far a state is expected to impose obligations on business entities concerning activities within their supply chains. In particular, the change in language from business relationships to contractual relationships [...] may limit corporate responsibility for supply chain management to the first subcontractors, although some maintain the opposite interpretation' (Kirkebø and Langford, 2020, p. 185).

The most recent Third Revised Draft from 2022 still does not mention supply chains, but switched its language back from contractual to business relations, specifying the latter in Article 1.5 as:

> any relationship between natural or legal persons, including State and non-State entities, to conduct business activities, including those activities conducted through affiliates, subsidiaries, agents, suppliers, partnerships, joint venture, beneficial proprietorship, or any other structure or relationship as provided under the domestic law of the State, including activities undertaken by electronic means.

This shift indicates that the disappearance of the term 'supply chains' does not simply represent an evasion of the topic. Rather, targeting 'business relations' can be read as an acknowledgement of the networked and informal ties in and beyond supply chains—which comes with its own regulation challenges. A closer look at the input side of the process that resulted in the draft treaties provides a more detailed understanding of the relation between the regulation of supply chains and human rights. These are mostly visible in the relevance, the measures and the challenges of supply chain regulation (SCR) from a human rights perspective.

4.3.2   Supply Chains' Relevance for Human Rights

The documents that address supply chains and their regulation explore whether (and why) supply chains need to be addressed from a human rights perspective. They discuss this question of relevance in terms of the effects of supply chains on human rights and the effects of SCR. The discussion is rather dichotomous, demonstrating a clear separation between the proponents and opponents of SCR.

Opponents of regulating supply chains for human rights violations downplay the prevalence of supply chains more generally: 'Indeed, according to the ILO World Employment Social Outlook 2015, only 20.6% of the global workforce is linked to Global Supply Chains (ILO WESO, page 132)' (Business\ IOE et al. joint written contribution: 3). They argue that if any detrimental effects on human rights emerge, supply chains play a secondary role compared to national economies, national jurisdictions, informal labor, and corruption. The International Organisation of Employers (IOE) argues:

> There are unquestionably working conditions in some cross-border supply chains that are unacceptable and that urgently need to be addressed just as there are for wholly domestic supply chains. The International Organisation of Employers has always been highly vocal in condemning unacceptable forms of work, and will continue to take this stance, referring particularly to the 1998 ILO Declaration on Fundamental Principles and Rights at Work and the 2014 Forced Labour Protocol. However, decent work challenges and negative environmental impacts in global

supply chains or investment projects are not unique to cross-border supply chains, but reflect general challenges in the local environment, such as a high prevalence of informality, ineffective governmental inspection, a lack of governance frameworks, high levels of corruption, and ineffective judiciary systems. The cross-border flow of goods, services and investment does not pose a unique challenge to decent work and sustainable development (Business\IOE Panel I: 1).

In a second major argument, opponents such as the BIAC, the Business and Industry Advisory Committee to the Organisation for Economic Co-operation and Development (OECD) underline the positive effects of supply chains:

Cross-border supply chains have been ladders of development and instrumental in bringing economic and social progress in industrialised, emerging and developing countries. Cross-border exchange fosters economic growth and creates jobs including by lifting people's chances of getting a foothold in the world of formal work. It promotes technological progress, enhances productivity, stimulates innovation that leads to skills-upgrading, and contributes to the reduction of poverty. Studies show that many jobs created in global supply chains provide better working conditions in a number of developing countries than jobs in purely domestic supply chains or work in the informal sector (Business \BIAC et al. written contribution: 5).

This argument contrasts with those made by SCR proponents. They emphasize the broad prevalence of supply chains, which account for 60–80% of global economic relations and trade, and underline the detrimental effects of supply chains on human rights. In particular, they address regulation and enforcement gaps, weak state agency, tax evasion, indecent working conditions, violations of workers' rights including the right to organize and bargain, informal work (which some opponents consider beyond the reach of supply chains) and the exploitation of vulnerable minorities.

TNCs [transnational corporations] could potentially help creating jobs and support economic and social development but the current model of trade, with the majority of trade tied to global value chain in highly competitive low cost markets means jobs created by TNCS often fall short of decent working standards. In fact, a recent study by the ITUC [International Trade Union Confederation] of 50 major corporations revealed that 94% of the workforce had no direct employment relationship, which makes them extra vulnerable to exploitation and abuses. The jobs created by transnational corporations (TNCs) are precarious. Cost pressures from global buyers mean that supply or value chain related employment is often insecure, involves poor working conditions and frequently fundamental human (including labour) rights violations. Indeed, forced labour, child labour, anti-union discrimination, forced overtime, unpaid wages and hazardous workplaces are common in global value chains (Unions\UNI Global Union' [Christy Hoffman] Presentation Panel I: 1)

With regard to the effects of SCR, proponents argue that stronger regulation mechanisms would combat the negative effects of supply chains, strengthen human rights protection and facilitate access to remedy for victims of human rights violations.

Opponents of regulation caution against the negative impacts of SCR, which they argue would harm not only individual companies, but also economic growth, economically or politically weak states from the Global South and brand-sensitive parent companies.

This demonstrates how diametrically opposed the discussion over the relevance of SCR is: most actors argue only either for or against it. This dichotomy is mirrored in the types of actors that participate in the treaty process. The majority of documents that oppose SCR are authored by business actors, whereas non-governmental organizations (NGOs) and unions submitted the majority of those in favor of SCR. Businesses are the only type of actor that has produced no documents advocating SCR. Unions are the only type that has not argued against SCR. States demonstrate a mixed, unclear or neutral stance towards SCR. For example, they may take positions that acknowledge problems in supply chains, but do not recognize the necessity of further regulation through a treaty.[5]

While unions submitted only 1.4% of the documents—which confirms the institutional divide discussed above—they address SCR in nearly all of them. By contrast, NGOs authored 53.9% of the documents analyzed, but only one third of them demand SCR. Hence actors that focus on labor rights most prominently advocate the regulation of supply chains. This may be because NGOs focus on a wider range of issue areas, which results in the differentiation of tasks and issues. Business actors address supply chains in nearly half of their contributions (which make up 5.3% of the documents), most of which strongly oppose SCR, while a few remain neutral. States (which generated 20.6% of the documents) address supply chains in one sixth of their statements. State documents proposing SCR (9.8%) outweigh those that oppose it (0.5%) and even those with mixed stances (5.7%).

4.3.3   SCR Measures from a Human Rights Perspective

SCR proponents suggest a variety of mechanisms and instruments to regulate supply chains from a human rights perspective. The most common are extending jurisdictions, lifting the corporate veil, establishing a duty of care, monitoring and sanctioning, remedy, reversing the burden of proof and increasing transparency.

Demands to extend jurisdictions aim to reduce the barriers to prosecuting companies and their suppliers in order to adjudicate, extend and enforce legislation beyond a state's domestic realm. Such demands may suggest abolishing or at least limiting the use of the doctrine forum non conveniens, which allows courts to decline adjudicating a case when another, apparently more convenient, court is at hand. Jurisdiction-related demands also seek to allow corporations to be tried both where they operate (host state) and where they are based (home state). According to SCR proponents, this would allow host state subsidiaries to be involved as co-defendants in claims against the parent company. It would also enable civil claims against subsidiaries, wherever they are based, and clarify which substantive civil law applies in cross-border cases. The Maastricht Principles on Extraterritorial Obligations of States in the Area of Economic, Social and Cultural Rights are regularly interpreted as providing a basis for home state responsibilities. Demands to extend jurisdictions do not rely on establishing direct business responsibilities; instead, they advocate the creation and extension of state-based legal mechanisms so that companies can be prosecuted without governance gaps.

Another measure that is invoked to enhance legal prosecution is to lift the corporate veil that allows companies to be treated as separate legal entities, which can help parent companies avoid liability for the actions of their subsidiaries abroad. Given the high prevalence of interdependence and linkages in supply chains, SCR proponents demand that companies connected through supply chains must be treated as a single economic unit:

> To improve access to remedy in the home countries, the treaty should finally require States to abolish the corporate veil and develop legal approaches to hold parent companies accountable for human rights abuses by their subsidiaries. For instance, the treaty should recognize all companies of a group as one company and include a presumption of parent company liability. To avoid regulatory loopholes, the future instrument should also clarify the condition under which supply chain liability should arise (NGOs\Brot für die Welt et al. Panel VI: 1).

The overall aim of lifting the corporate veil is to establish parent company liability for the entire supply chain. Since there is disagreement over when and how to lift this veil, proponents such as the International Network for Economic, Social and Cultural Rights (ESCR-Net) and the Fédération internationale des ligues des droits de l'Homme (FIDH) suggest focusing on the question of liability for human rights:

> Recognise the Principle of Enterprise Liability: Under this option, the treaty may encourage states to recognise all companies of a group as one 'enterprise' for the purposes of litigation involving human rights. This would avoid the need for litigation as to whether the corporate veil should be lifted or not, thus brining more legal certainty for all parties. [...] This option should also encourage companies of a group to consider human rights issues more holistically for the entire group, rather than move risky or hazardous businesses to distant or under-funded subsidiaries' (NGOs\ESCR-Net and FIDH briefing paper 4 [Parent company liability] d: 3).

Another approach to dealing with the separation of legal entities is to establish a duty of care, which obligates a parent company to step in if its subsidiary cannot meet its liabilities. Demands refer to both narrow and broad models, which include only direct subsidiaries of a company or whole supply chains, respectively. The documents refer to the tort law parent company duty of care as it has been established in the United Kingdom. Duty of care even provides a measure that reconciles opposition to a full removal of the corporate veil:

> The treaty should therefore not require abolishing the principle of separate legal personality even if many scholars used to consider piercing its corporate veil as the only possibility to hold the dominant company accountable. However, as the French law and the English tort law show, it is also possible to establish a liability regime for dominant companies in linking their duty of care to the control or influence capacity over the dominated companies (Individuals\Paul Mougeolle_PHD Candidate_submission to draft: 7).

Demands for monitoring and sanctioning point out that it is not sufficient to establish laws on SCR; companies, states and other actors must be obliged to actively monitor its implementation (e.g., via periodic evaluation and follow-up mechanisms) and states must be able to sanction companies for non-compliance, including civil (financial) and criminal sanctions (e.g., the ability to dissolve a company). SCR proponents argue that monitoring mechanisms and penalties would not only help enforce implementation, but could also help prevent human rights violations.

The demand for access to remedy—which includes compensation and access to different forms of justice—focuses on helping the victims of human rights violations instead of prosecuting the perpetrators. Remedy is highly dependent on the other instruments, as it relies on establishing companies' liability and responsibility as well as effective state jurisdiction. It also relies on access to information and the lowering of legal and judicial barriers, such as the absence of class action mechanisms or the high costs of legal representation.

A measure to lower the barriers to remedy access is the reversal of the burden of proof, which is the subject of fierce discussions in the treaty process.

> [Human rights responsibility in supply chains] will not be easy to apply to situations where companies violated human rights, if the victim is required to prove the proximity of the parent company to the subsidiary or to the wrong behaviour or the failure of the parent company to undertake due diligence. The difficulty for victims to prove such elements is one of the most recurrent barriers that impede access to justice (NGOs\fidh_ Report (Comments on the Zero Draft): 20).

The measure of transparency refers to the links between companies and subsidiaries and is closely connected to the measure of access to such information. Due to the highly complex structures of companies and their relations with other companies, transparency creates the foundation for the other instruments—especially access to remedy, establishing liability and piercing the corporate veil—by revealing the links between tiers of a supply chain, which is necessary for establishing responsibility in the first place.

One proposal combines demands for transparency and monitoring with economic profitability:

> many corporates are seriously looking for more effective and automated system in monitoring and assessing compliance with such rules and regulations. [...] Basically, if every data on transactions of corporates is recorded on block-chain-based data-base which could not be altered retroactively and maintained publicly without any central control authority, the people whose human rights are harmed or violated could identify which organization is primarily responsible and make complaint electronically through smartphone (Individuals\Akihiko Morita_Professor_submission to draft: 3-4).

Transparency not only provides the basis for other instruments; it also relies on these other instruments to fully establish human rights responsibility in supply chains, such as a functioning jurisdiction and access to remedy.

The statements that generally oppose SCR partially demonstrate a lack of controversy over concrete measures. To be sure, opponents fiercely argue against making parent companies legally responsible for the actions of their subsidiaries. In addition to pointing out the negative economic effects of SCR presented above, they argue that companies would find ways to circumvent parent liability, and that this would complicate supply chains and forms of legal liability instead of improving them. Extraterritorial jurisdiction is also fiercely disputed. Opponents fear that increasing the liability of parent companies and home states would decrease the pressure on subsidiaries and host states, thereby simply transferring—rather than strengthening—responsibility.

Nevertheless, with regard to the extension of jurisdictions, opponents agree that states should take on more responsibilities, even though they disagree on their implementation and enforcement. What is more, opponents either do not address or do not oppose transparency, remedy and monitoring measures.[6] This might be due to a lack of attention, but this does not sufficiently explain why opponents do not react to such popular demands. If the lack of opposition to transparency, remedy and monitoring indicates a lack of controversy, these instruments might provide a basis for establishing human rights responsibility in supply chains that is acceptable to those who otherwise resist further regulation.

4.3.4   Challenges to Regulating Supply Chains and Business Relations

The documents analyzed here pay particular attention to the challenges of regulating supply chains from a human rights perspective. SCR proponents and opponents both acknowledge the complexity of supply chains; they discuss companies' influence and address the scope of business relations beyond supply chains. Yet, both again draw different conclusions.

The complexity of supply chains is one of the major arguments put forward by SCR opponents. They argue that business relations in supply chains are too complex to be covered by a treaty:

> Global supply chains are understood to be 'complex, diverse and fragmented' and they are constantly changing in response to economic factors and market conditions. Buyers do not control their full supply chains and their ability to influence the business conduct of a supplier largely depends on the buyer's market position (Business\ IOE_Panel V: 2).

Proponents agree that supply chains are complex, yet they search for ways to address that complexity. With varying degrees of emphasis, they differentiate chains and their tiers according to contractual relationships, franchises, common goals, common management with a division of tasks, common shareholders, subsidiaries, subcontractors, other suppliers, contractors, licensees, intra-firm or inter-firm, regional or global affiliates, and co-contracting parties, as well as clients. Additionally, they propose including investors, banks, loans, hedge funds, pension funds and philanthropic funds. Throughout, proponents highlight the transnational nature of supply chains, which poses one of the greatest challenges to their regulation.

By contrast, opponents argue that the transnational element of supply chains is negligible. They instead emphasize the national character of supply chains and refer to their regulation at the state level. According to this perspective, regulation should take place strictly on the domestic rather than the global level.

For both opponents and proponents, the question of companies' influence over the tiers in their supply chain is pivotal. Proponents invoke relations of formal and informal control. Given the complexity of these relations, they put forward the need to define and apply control thoroughly and comprehensively, emphasizing that control applies beyond ownership:

> Although parent company control over a subsidiary or joint venture can be evident in paper and from corporate management, only in exceptional circumstances have courts imposed liability on the parent company under this criterion. This prob-

lematic reveals the need for a specific definition of control (NGOs\fidh_ Report (Comments on the Zero Draft): 19).

We propose: 'the control of the parent company over its value chain can be direct, indirect, financial, economic or otherwise' (NGOs\FoEI_Panel V (Art.3;4) (transl.): 1: 1477 - 1: 1935).

This description includes the supply chain – as long as it is controlled by the TNC – as a part of the TNC, even if this control is not exercised via ownership or holding controlling shares of the supply chain company, but simply because the supply chain totally depends economically for its output and/or input on 'the brain' (NGOs\FIAN International_Report 2017: 6).

[C]ontrol can be exerted through non-equity relationships, such as licensing, franchising and subcontracting through supply chains. Also, when ownership structures are complex, tribunals look beyond equity ownership and consider other indicators of control such as involvement in substantial business activity. In all cases, control is the key, for in control lies responsibility. It is through control that a TNC or foreign investor shapes decision- making, sets policies and practice, and has ultimate responsibility to respect human rights in companywide operations (Individuals\ Khalil Hamdani_Lahore School of Economics_Panel IV: 2: 2190 - 2: 2837).

Control is not only invoked as an empirical fact that should be covered by SCR; it is also advanced as a demand: companies should be obliged to control their suppliers. Here, control is invoked to strengthen business relations and therefore responsibility in supply chains to circumvent regulatory gaps resulting from, for example, restricted extraterritorial state jurisdiction. Opponents reject such demands, arguing that if parent companies had greater control over their suppliers, this would lead to 'stricter policeman-like policies in their cross-border supply chains' (Business\IOE_Panel III (Art. 9): 1).

As an alternative to the parameter of control, proponents refer to the concept of leverage from the UNGPs. They underline the need to define leverage in order to establish business responsibilities in supply chains. Remarkably, opponents of the principles also invoke leverage:

The UNGPs recognize that companies do not control every dimension of these relationships, so they introduce the concept of leverage. Where people's human rights are adversely affected by activities in a company's value chain, the company's responsibility is to use its leverage to try to improve those people's situation. Where the leverage is insufficient the company is expected to try and increase it, perhaps in collaboration with other companies or different stakeholders. I venture to predict that this is where business can make its single biggest contribution to the people part of the sustainable development agenda (Business\IOE_follow-up response to elements: 5).

While opponents agree with proponents that leverage can constitute business responsibility in supply chains, they are eager to limit the meaning and extent of leverage:

> For example, small and medium-sized enterprises (SMEs) often have limited lever-age over their suppliers. In other scenarios, large TNCs may find themselves having limited leverage when they source only a small amount of a supplier's production, or when the supplier has a monopoly, or when the supplier is actually a much bigger company than the TNC. Furthermore, it is often impossible or impractical, either economically or logistically, to control all suppliers and subcontractors. These com-plexities and limitations have been recognized in many Government-backed instru-ments, such as the UNGPs and the OECD Guidelines for Multinational Enterprises, which recognize the practical limitations on business enterprises to effect a change in their supplier's behaviour. These limitations relate to product characteristics, the number of suppliers, the structure and complexity of the supply chain, the market position of the enterprise vis-à-vis its suppliers or other entities in the supply chain (Business\IOE_Panel V: 2).

Given the difficulties of establishing control or leverage in supply chains, some proponents seek to establish human rights responsibilities in business relations beyond supply chains. In its most extensive form, this includes all kinds of business relations and associations:

> The Treaty should ensure that the regulation of TNC-OBE activity reflects the exist-ing conditions and lived experiences of people globally, requiring States to, among other things: Address in detail the particularly complex regulatory challenges posed by TNCs, including in relation to subsidiary companies, supply chains, and all other business enterprises otherwise associated with their operations, products or services through their business relationships (NGOs\ESCR-Net written_contribution: 4).

To further define the scope and meaning of business relations beyond supply chains, proponents invoke two principles from the UNGPs. The first is cor-porate complicity, which defines business relations as including entities other than business actors, such as repressive states:

> The concept of 'corporate complicity' is a key way to understand and assess the extent to which corporations should be held responsible for their own contributions to acts of third parties, such as governments, the military and security providers, as well as subsidiaries and other businesses in corporate supply chains (NGOs\ ESCR-Net and FIDH_Report 2016 (Ten Key Proposals): 74).

The second principle from the UNGPs used to extend business relations beyond supply chains is due diligence:

> The UNGPs also note that business enterprises have a due diligence responsibility in relation to both their own actions (where they must avoid causing or contributing

to adverse human rights impacts and address such impacts when they occur), and the actions of third parties (including business partners, entities in its supply chain, and any other non-State or State entity directly linked to its business operations, products or services, (where they should seek to prevent or mitigate adverse human rights impacts even if they have not contributed to those impacts) (NGOs\ESCR-Net and FIDH_Report 2016 (Ten Key Proposals): 58).

Opponents strictly reject the extension of human rights responsibilities for business relations beyond supply chains. However, the notions of complicity and due diligence, alongside the concept of leverage, point to business relations beyond direct and vertical chains, offering alternative definitions of control. Opponents even refer to due diligence as an instrument that helps avoid overly broad definitions of business relations. This makes due diligence a shared concept that both opponents and proponents invoke to strengthen their arguments.

In sum, opponents and proponents agree that supply chains and their regulation are a multi-faceted and complex issue that needs to be approached with great care, but disagree over the implications and conclusions that can be drawn from this complexity. Opponents argue that supply chains are too complex to establish human rights responsibility, while proponents note that this complexity causes regulatory gaps, and highlight the need to establish regulation and responsibilities from a human rights perspective.

4.4 FRACTURED LINKS IN REGULATION: BUSINESS POWER, BINDINGNESS AND POLICY LEVEL

The analysis of the treaty process indicates strong links between the global regulation of supply chains and human rights, yet these links are fractured. While these fractures are partly marked by controversies between supporters and opponents of SCR, they do not represent clear and one-sided dichotomies. Rather, the ways that links and fractures interact demonstrate their potential to strengthen SCR from a human rights perspective—as well as the challenges of doing so. This is particularly visible in three regulatory dimensions that this section discusses in turn: business power, the bindingness of regulation, and the policy level of regulation.

4.4.1 Business Power

With regard to capturing business power, particularly businesses' ability to control their supply chains and suppliers, proponents assume that companies exercise strong control not only over their own subsidiaries, but also over suppliers which are not owned by the focal firm and with whom they are only related via contracts or even more informal ties. This is based on an understanding of power that goes beyond legal and formal ties and takes its multiple faces into account. These include economic power relating to a company's size, resources and hierarchical ties, as well as different types of dependence and interdependence (Gereffi et al., 2005; Wickert et al., 2016), the power to influence agenda setting, and the power to affect norms and ideas (Fuchs, 2004; Mende, 2022). Remarkably, even the narrowest definition of economic power allows companies to influence suppliers that they do not own (e.g., via the threat of cancelling their contracts or relations).

Opponents, by contrast, generally describe the extent of business power as rather low and argue that it is the demanded regulation of supply chains that would accumulate business power in an unwanted way. Proponents, however, claim that this is already the case in (unregulated) supply chains: companies assert power in political, societal and governance matters, and they can easily compete with (if not overrule) other actors—even states. This 'provides lead companies with opportunities for control and influence' (Millington, 2008, p. 363), including the agency to assume human rights responsibility.

Opponents and proponents agree that the topic's complexity presents a major challenge to SCR from a human rights perspective. For both sides, the principles of due diligence and leverage as framed in the UNGPs play an important role in tackling business power within and beyond supply chains. These principles acknowledge the different kinds of relations between companies, and take economic as well as agenda-setting and discursive powers into account.

4.4.2   The Bindingness of Regulation

The bindingness of regulation is a regulatory dimension that acts as the direct counterpart to common references to due diligence and leverage, because it is at this point that proponents and opponents of SCR diverge. Opponents use the principle of leverage to concede certain forms of influence that businesses might yield over suppliers. However, they emphasize the limits of such influence, its difference to real power and its foundation in friendly relations. They argue that all of this requires that leverage not be used as a basis for binding regulation. They treat leverage and due diligence as useful tools as long as they operate on a non-binding basis. This does not mean that these tools do not affect business behavior. On the contrary, their establishment in the UNGPs, as well as the more recent initiatives on due diligence as in the European Union, have moved the business community tremendously. Yet opponents struggle against their juridification, which causes them to argue against the treaty and SCR. Proponents, by contrast, refer to the principles of due diligence and leverage as decisive normative steps in the development of business respon-sibilities for human rights. While proponents of SCR also identify success in certain non-binding forms of business responsibility, they consider SCR regulation as incomplete from a human rights perspective as long as it only contains non-binding forms.

4.4.3   The Policy Level of Regulation

The third regulatory dimension relates to the policy level of regulation. The analysis shows that debates over who is responsible for human rights in supply chains are pluralist, not dichotomous. While they are marked by a divide between business responsibilities and state responsibilities (i.e., whether states or companies should be held responsible for human rights violations), there is a significant overlap in considering states as duty bearers. Proponents do not simply or exclusively demand that companies take the lead in SCR; quite the opposite: the proposed SCR measures are closely connected (but not limited) to state-based action. Opponents also consider the state to be the duty bearer, fearing that duties might otherwise be directly imposed on companies. Thus, both positions can be said to link to a complementary model of human rights responsibility in which state and business duties may interact. This is regularly referred to as a 'smart mix' in the context of the UNGPs.

Opponents, however, insist on the state level of regulation in a way that corresponds to their argument that human rights violations in supply chains are usually a domestic rather than a global issue. Proponents, by contrast, highlight the transnational reach of business power as the main challenge of regulating supply chains from a human rights perspective, as it enables com-panies to exploit the gaps in global regulation, allowing them to choose the location of their production, their suppliers or their registration according to local human rights and supply chain laws (or the lack thereof). Furthermore, the transnational agency of (global) companies, as well as their transnational business relations, make it more difficult to determine which actor in the supply chain is responsible for a human rights violation, and to link the vio-lation to a state that is willing and able to prosecute the violator and remedy the victim (Mende, 2020b). The latter also entails involving different legal systems and jurisdictions that need to be reconciled (Millington, 2008). The growing complexity of business relations and the legal forms that business enterprises can take exacerbate these challenges (Dicken, 2011; Mikler, 2013). Notably, the draft treaties do not circumvent or supersede domestic legislation, but rather emphasize states' roles and duties. Such responsibilities entail the development of national laws and duties for companies at the domestic level, as well as the means to prosecute and hold companies accountable. The goal is for international policy to begin targeting the gaps of domestic policy in addressing the global relevance and challenges of supply chains.

4.5   CONCLUSION

This chapter characterizes the relationship between the global regulation of supply chains and human rights as linked but fractured. It shows that their global institutionalization is divergent, but partly merges in the issue area of business and human rights. It reveals how the relevance, measures and challenges of supply chain regulation link to human rights, and how the fractures within these links indicate both the potential of and the challenges for supply chain regulation from a human rights perspective. Identifying three linked, yet fractured regulatory dimensions (business power, bindingness and policy level), this chapter argues in favor of further developing and applying the concepts of control, due diligence and leverage. Ultimately, it shows that the regulation of supply chains can (and must) be discussed within a larger framework that takes human rights as well as power relations at different policy levels into account, including that of and between states and companies, as well as other stakeholders.

NOTES

1. At the same time, the question of whether only trans-border or also domestic supply chains are relevant for human rights is a matter of fierce discussion in the treaty process, as shown below.
2. ILO (2015), compared to 296 million workers in 1995, and a peak of 500 million in 2007 ILO (2015).
3. The ILO became a specialized UN agency in 1946.
4. I applied an explanatory qualitative content analysis (Mende 2022), which integrates qualitative content analysis with elements of grounded theory in three steps. First, I sorted the material deductively, coding all statements that relate to supply chains. A second round of inductive coding further developed the dimensions and sub-categories of supply chain-related statements. In a third round of axial coding, the dimensions and sub-categories were further analyzed in terms of their interrelations, reasons and justifications. Quotes from the documents are marked with the type of actor, the document title as used in the IGWG or publication forum, and the page number of the quote.
5. In some instances, opponents acknowledge the importance of certain measures and defer responsibility for them from the company to the state level.
6. Another example of mixed positions are statements that describe national laws and mechanisms of SCR without clarifying whether these should be expanded to regulate supply chains globally or whether they would make an international treaty redundant, for example.

REFERENCES

Alston, P. (ed.) (2005). *Non-state actors and human rights*. Oxford University Press.

Andreopoulos, G.J., Arat, Z.F.K., & Juviler, P.H. (eds.) (2006). *Non-state actors in the human rights universe*. Kumarian Press.

Arnold, D.G., & Bowie, N.E. (2007). Respect for workers in global supply chains: Advancing the debate over sweatshops. *Business Ethics Quarterly*, 17(1), 135–145.

Avery, C. (2000). Business and human rights in a time of change. In: Kamminga, M.T., & Zia-Zarifi, S. (eds.), *Liability of multinational corporations under international law*, 17–74, Kluwer Law International.

Barrientos, S., Mayer, F., Pickles, J., & Posthuma, A. (2011). Decent work in global production networks: Framing the policy debate. *International Labour Review*, 150(3-4), 297–317.

Clapham, A. (1993). *Human rights in the private sphere*. Clarendon Press.

Clarke, T., & Boersma, M. (2017). The governance of global value chains: Unresolved human rights, environmental and ethical dilemmas in the Apple supply chain. *Journal of Business Ethics*, 143(1), 111–131.

Crane, A., LeBaron, G., Allain, J., & Behbahani, L. (2017). Governance gaps in eradicating forced labor: From global to domestic supply chains. *Regulation & Governance*, 35(1), 1.

Craven, M.C.R. (1998). *The international covenant on economic, social, and cultural rights: A perspective on its development*. Clarendon Press.

Dicken, P. (2011). *Global shift, sixth edition: Mapping the changing contours of the world economy*. Guilford Press.

Ebert, F.C. (n.d.). Unpublished manuscript.

Fenwick, C.F., & Novitz, T. (2010). *Human rights at work: Perspectives on law and regulation*. Hart Publishing.

Fuchs, D. (2004). The role of business in global governance. In: Schirm, S.A. (ed.), *New rules for global markets: Public and private governance in the world economy*, 133–154, Palgrave Macmillan.

Gereffi, G., Humphrey, J., & Sturgeon, T. (2005). The governance of global value chains. *Review of International Political Economy*, 12(1), 78–104.

Gold, S., Trautrims, A., & Trodd, Z. (2015). Modern slavery challenges to supply chain management. *Supply Chain Management: An International Journal*, 20(5), 485–94.

ILO (2015). World employment and social outlook 2015: The changing nature of jobs. International Labour Office, Geneva.

Kirkebø, T.L., & Langford, M. (2020). Ground-breaking: An empirical assessment of the Draft Business and Human Rights Treaty. *American Journal of International Law*, 114, 179–85.

Krisch, N. (ed.) (2021). *Entangled legalities beyond the state*. Cambridge University Press.

Locke, R., Amengual, M., & Mangla, A. (2009). Virtue out of necessity: Compliance, commitment, and the improvement of labor conditions in global supply chains. *Politics & Society*, 37(3), 319–351.

Mantouvalou, V. (2012). Are labour rights human rights? *European Labour Law Journal*, 3(2), 151–172.

Mende, J. (2020a). *Dataset binding treaty on business and human rights*. Harvard Dataverse.

Mende, J. (2020b). The public, the private, and the business-societal: A threefold approach to business responsibility for human rights. In: Stohl, M., & Brysk, A. (eds.), *A research agenda for human rights*, 155–172, Edward Elgar Publishing.

Mende, J. (2022). Extended qualitative content analysis: Researching the United Nations and other international institutions. *Qualitative Research Journal*, 22(3), 340–353.

Mende, J. (2023). Business authority in global governance: Companies beyond public and private roles. *Journal of International Political Theory*, 19(2), 200–220.

Mikler, J. (ed.) (2013). *The handbook of global companies*. Wiley-Blackwell.

Millington, A. (2008). Responsibility in the supply chain. In: Crane, A. (ed.), *The Oxford handbook of corporate social responsibility*, 363–383, Oxford University Press.

Morrison, J. (2011). An overview of current practice and policy relating to business activities and human rights: Some of the implications for corporate 'rule-making'. In: Pies, I., & Koslowski, P. (eds.), *Corporate citizenship and new governance: The political role of corporations*, 7–18, Springer.

Pagnattaro, M.A. (2014). Labor rights are human rights: Sustainability initiatives and trade policy. In: Bird, R.C., Cahoy, D.R., Prenkert, J.D. (eds.), *Law, business and human rights: Bridging the gap*, 143–170, Edward Elgar Publishing.

Ramasastry, A. (2015). Corporate social responsibility versus business and human rights: Bridging the gap between responsibility and accountability. *Journal of Human Rights*, 14(2), 237–59.

Saner, R., & You, L. (2020). Labor rights as human rights. In: Rubin, N., & Flores, R. (eds.), *The Cambridge handbook of psychology and human rights*, 105–120, Cambridge University Press.

Scherrer, C. (2017). Introduction. In: Scherrer, C. (ed.), *Enforcement instruments for social human rights along supply chains*, 1–5, Rainer Hampp Verlag.

Schutter, O. de, Eide, A., Khalfan, A., Orellana, M., Salomon, M., & Seiderman, I. (2012). Commentary to the Maastricht Principles on Extraterritorial Obligations of States in the Area of Economic, Social and Cultural Rights. *Human Rights Quarterly*, 34(4), 1084–1169.

Servais, J.-M., & van Goethem, V. (2016). *International Labour Organization (ILO)*. Wolters Kluwer.

Steffek, J., & Hahn, K. (eds.) (2010). *Evaluating transnational NGOs: Legitimacy, accountability, representation*. Palgrave Macmillan.

UNCTAD (2013). *World investment report 2013: Global value chains: investment and trade for development*. United Nations.

UNCTAD (2018). *World investment report 2018: Investment and new industrial policies*. United Nations.

Wettstein, F. (2009). *Multinational corporations and global justice: The human rights obligations of a quasi-governmental institution*. Stanford Business Books.

Wickert, C., Scherer, A.G., & Spence, L.J. (2016). Walking and talking corporate social responsibility: Implications of firm size and organizational cost. *Journal of Management Studies*, 53(7), 1169–1196.

5. Understanding modern slavery through the lens of behavioral ethics

Mehrdokht Pournader, Andrew P. Kach and Vikram Bhakoo

5.1 INTRODUCTION

The supply chain management literature has been more progressive compared to its counterparts in the business and management disciple in publishing scholarship on modern slavery (Caruana et al., 2021). Yet, despite this growing interest, which we believe is encouraging, Caruana et al. (2021) describe the state of the field of modern slavery research as 'significantly, and disappointingly, underdeveloped' (p. 251). Studies conducted across different contexts such as fishing (Wilhelm et al., 2020), construction (Trautrims et al., 2021), fashion (Benstead et al., 2021; Meshram et al., 2021), consumer electronics (Nolan and Boersma, 2019) and in different regions of the world do indeed highlight that despite strong impetuous to tackle this wicked problem, this crime has persisted. In addition, despite the theoretical and practical efforts to reduce modern slavery in supply chains, such efforts have not yet been successful (Yawar and Seuring, 2017; Simpson et al., 2021; Villena et al., 2021) and modern slavery continues to thrive in global supply chains.

Taking one step back, the literature has shown that controlling mechanisms and codes of conduct in place to punish unethical behavior are not very effective (Bazerman and Banaji, 2004; Schminke et al., 2014). The consistent rise in cases of modern slavery in global supply chains, and subsequent complacency of buying firms toward these cases, can be considered as ethical failures. These ethical failures have been the common denominator for business ethics studies posing the question of how they can be managed and regulated for effective mitigation (De Cremer et al., 2010b).

These concerns prompted us to look beyond modern slavery, supply chain management, and business ethics to introduce behavioral ethics as a promising avenue that can be adopted to enrich insights on modern slavery in supply chains. The main difference between behavioral ethics and business ethics is that traditionally business ethics models and theories have been based on a normative and prescriptive approach, mandating what ethical behavior should look, sound, and feel like (Cremer and Moore, 2020; Trevino and Weaver, 1994). However, this normative approach is not overly useful, especially when people understand what ethical behavior entails but still choose the unethical alternative. It should come as no surprise that global buying firms experiencing modern slavery in their immediate supply chains are aware of their inaction or failure in addressing these unethical cases, yet still show some degree of complacency toward modern slavery. Perhaps one of the most notable examples is the ongoing complacency of global fashion and clothing brands toward their workers' health and safety despite the Rana Plaza incident (Chan, 2021). If we take this at face value, then the main question is whether we consider these firms and people working for them to all be complicit in this crime. Or is it more realistic to think about the context in which these decision makers make a trade-off between internal rewards of complacency toward modern slavery (e.g., monetary, psychological, job security) and being unethical?

If we consider the fact that people with good intentions are still capable of doing bad things and move beyond the normative view of business ethics, then we enter the realm of behavioral ethics. What follows in the remainder of this chapter is a brief introduction to behavioral ethics accompanied by a discussion of key frameworks and theories associated with it that can be applied to studies surrounding modern slavery in supply chains. It is worth noting that similar to behavioral operations (Bendoly et al., 2010), behavioral ethics functions at cognitive, social, and group levels; thereby, we will aim at introducing relevant behavioral factors and theories on all these three levels that can be applied to the study of modern slavery in supply chains.

5.2   WHAT IS BEHAVIORAL ETHICS?

Despite some earlier definitions of behavioral ethics by Treviño et al. (2006) and Tenbrunsel and Smith-Crowe (2008), we borrow the definition of behavioral ethics from Bazerman and Gino (2012, p. 90) as follows:

> behavioral ethics [is] the study of systematic and predictable ways in which individuals make ethical decisions and judge the ethical decisions of others, ways that are at odds with intuition and the benefits of the broader society.

At the core of behavioral ethics is the assumption that ordinary individuals frequently behave unethically (Gerlach et al., 2019). This engagement in unethical behavior is not necessarily done by bad people and/or deliberately (Moore and Gino, 2015; Nieuwenboer et al., 2017), hence highlighting the need to understand the 'ways' in which this type of unethical behavior occurs. The ways through which (good) employees adopt unethical behavior falls within the domain of behavioral ethics studies (Treviño et al., 2006; De Cremer et al., 2010a; Bazerman and Gino, 2012; De Cremer and Tenbrunsel, 2012; Moore and Gino, 2015; De Cremer and Vandekerckhove, 2017; Cremer and Moore, 2020).

The origins of behavioral ethics can be traced back to behavioral economics, organizational behavior, psychology, and management and business ethics (Cremer and Moore, 2020). Similar to ideas from behavioral economics and behavioral operations, behavioral ethics is concerned with the deviations of individuals from logic and rationality, especially when faced with making ethical decisions. Unlike behavioral economics and behavioral operations, where the ultimate goal is understanding how or why deviations from rationality harm the self-interest of individuals, behavioral ethics studies how self-interest can be the underlying factor behind unethical behavior (Cremer and Moore, 2020). Self-interest can indeed be the main driver for people subconsciously gravitating toward unethical behavior (Ariely and Jones, 2012). In fact, one of the earliest studies on behavioral ethics by Loewenstein (1996) investigates how behaving unethically can be a mental trade off where the decision maker's well-being (i.e., self-interest) is prioritized, which in turn produces harm for others. Such mental trade-offs are hypothetically quite prevalent in modern slavery studies—for example, how employees will remain silent and not 'blow the whistle' when they witness their peers harmed within the work environment, as to not to get singled out by their employer.

In the following section, we will investigate a number of frameworks and theories from behavioral ethics and their applications to modern slavery studies in supply chains. We have proposed two broad categories of 'cognitive factors' and 'organizational and situational factors' in which we selectively discuss some important topics for modern slavery studies in supply chains. While cognitive factors relate to behavioral models surrounding cognitive psychology and individual ethical decision-making procedure, organizational factors are concerned with organizational settings that affect individual or group ethical decision making, and situational factors discuss context-specific factors that are not necessarily organizational but can impact ethical decision making.

5.3   COGNITIVE FACTORS

5.3.1   Bounded Awareness and Bounded Ethicality

Bounded awareness is when individuals are so hyper-focused on something (e.g., end goals, specific details, monetary gains) that they become oblivious to available and relevant information during their decision-making process (Bazerman and Chugh, 2006; Chugh and Bazerman, 2007). A famous example of bounded awareness is the basketball game video by Simons and Chabris (1999), where viewers of the video were so focused on the game that they did not notice the person in the gorilla costume passing through the court. In addition to people failing to take into account crucial information during decision making, they also overlook alternative options and other stakeholders involved in the decision-making process (Bazerman, 2014; Bazerman and Sezer, 2016).

Bounded ethicality is the psychological process through which an individual engages in unethical behavior that is not aligned with their own ethical beliefs (Chugh et al., 2005). There are similarities between bounded ethicality, bounded awareness, and bounded rationality in that a certain level of cognitive shortcoming is involved which results in decisions or actions that are not preferred (e.g., if the cognitive shortcoming were revealed). Some examples of bounded ethicality in psychology and management consist of taking extra credit for group work, holding an overly positive view of one's self, and favoritism (Tenbrunsel et al., 2010; Bazerman and Moore, 2012).

Bounded ethicality also takes on more complex forms such as the recent Iuventa case, where 21 employees of two NGOs and a shipping company were indicted for illegally smuggling refugees into Italy in attempts to remove them from arguably worse conditions in Libya (Amnesty International, 2021).

Some psychological issues within bounded awareness that can further facilitate bounded ethicality and cause unethical behavior are outcome biases, slippery slopes, indirect blindness, and motivated blindness (we refer the readers to Bazerman and Sezer, 2016, for further information and detailed discussions on each psychological process). Here are some examples of each psychological issue related to modern slavery in supply chains:

- Outcome bias: Is modern slavery in supply chains condemned more harshly when it results in financial or reputational losses to the buying firm compared to when it saves on costs for the buying firm?
- Slippery slope: Are buying firms more forgiving of modern slavery discoveries at their supplier locations when they happen gradually versus abruptly?
- Indirect blindness: Are buying firms more forgiving of modern slavery incidents when engaging in subcontracting as compared to their immediate suppliers?
- Motivated blindness: Are buying firms more inclined to dismiss cases of modern slavery when it does not help and/or hurt their bottom line?

5.3.2 Moral Disengagement

Moral disengagement (Bandura, 1999) is a facet of social cognitive theory (Bandura, 1986; 1991) that explores how individuals disassociate from unethical decisions so they do not feel guilty. Moral disengagement is comprised of four loci or sets (behavioral, agency, outcomes, and victim) and eight cognitive mechanisms, each belonging to a certain set. Below are some examples of each cognitive mechanism applied to a supply chain-related modern slavery issue:

- Behavioral
  - Moral justification: 'It is okay if my supplier has minor cases of exploitation as long as it keeps them out of poverty'.
  - Euphemistic labelling: 'My supplier's employees are just a bit tired, and they should be fine after some rest'.
  - Advantageous comparison: 'Compared to the extreme cases of physical harm by other suppliers, a few overworked employees by my suppliers are negligible'.
- Agency
  - Displacement of responsibility: 'My suppliers cannot be blamed for modern slavery since they have been under pressure to deliver on time'.
  - Diffusion of responsibility: 'Considering the fact that everyone has some type of modern slavery somewhere in their supply chains, there is no reason we should be held to a higher standard'.
- Outcomes
  - Distortion of consequences: 'If a few of my suppliers' employees are exploited to deliver a multi-million project, it is no big deal'.
- Victim
  - Dehumanization: 'Workers of my suppliers in poor countries are not snowflakes and can tolerate harsh working conditions with minimum pay'.
  - Attribution of blame: 'If employees of my supplier are being punished physically or paid less than others then they have probably brought it on themselves'.

5.3.3 Neutralization

Under neutralization theory, which has its roots in criminology, individuals are able to neutralize certain traits or values which would typically inhibit them from engaging in unethical or illegal behavior (e.g., Polding, 2017; Matza, 2018). This has been argued to manifest through legitimizing structures where individuals believe that their actions were justified. These structures are 'denial of responsibility', where the individual believes that the situation was out of their control; 'denial of injury', where the individual believes that their actions did not cause any damages or harm; 'denial of the victim', where the individual believes that those impacted by the unethical behavior were deserving of it; 'condemnation of the condemners', where the individual believes that those condemning them of their unethical behavior are doing so out of enmity or malice; and 'appeal to higher loyalties', where the individual believes that the negative affect of the unethical behavior is outweighed by the good that it ultimately causes. More recently the following two structures were included which are 'defense of necessity', where the individual believes that their actions served a particular purpose (Minor, 1980), and 'metaphor of the ledger', where the individual believes that they have accomplished significant good enough to allow for some unethical behavior (Klockars, 1974; Minor, 1980).

Many of these legitimizing structures associated with neutralization share similarities with moral disengagement; one way to think about these theories working together is that moral disengagement operates alongside individuals engaging in unethical behavior and neutralization theory is how they justify or rationalize it afterwards. A recent example of neutralization includes indictments made against Starbucks for modern slavery conditions and child labor discovered at multiple coffee growing sites. Some level of responsibility by Starbucks is denied given that the suppliers are seen as outside the control of the firm; and moreover, 'fair trade' and C.A.R.E. standards have been implemented providing sufficient goodwill in attempts to achieve 99% levels of sustainability (e.g., so of course there will be some hiccups along the way).

5.3.4   Ethical Fading

Ethical fading is when individuals engage in a form of 'self-deception', where the ethical landscape associated with decision making is removed from the person's periphery in order to obtain a specific outcome or goal (Tenbrunsel and Messick, 2004). Similar to moral disengagement, where reality is 'restructured' in order to reduce the harmful nature of the action, ethical fading involves guilt minimization mechanics, often at the expense of others (Rees et al., 2019). Those engaging in ethical fading will often highly prioritize the outcome (e.g., winning a game) such that they begin to dismiss or remove ethics as part of the process. In global supply chains, an example of this is buying firms getting wrapped up in their competitive landscape to the point where their suppliers (and everyone working for them) are simply a means to 'beating out' the other players in the market. Cost becomes the primary focus, and ethics are seemingly secondary to negligible, leading to oversight in terms of workforce abuses, human rights violations, or otherwise at supplier locations. Along those lines, ethical fading is closely related to moral myopia, where individuals cannot see ethical issues clearly due to their reality becoming distorted or blurred. As an example, many major automotive and electronics manufacturers are reliant on lithium ion batteries. Cobalt, a rare earth metal and primary material in those batteries is mainly mined in the Democratic Republic of the Congo (circa 60% of the world's supply) where unsafe working conditions, human rights violations, and child labor is commonplace. There are similar examples surrounding tin mining in Indonesia; however, many firms justify their sourcing practices through growing manufacturing demands, cost pressures, and lack of transparency in the supply chain.

5.3.5   Actor-observer Bias

Another area impacting modern slavery related challenges in supply chains are situational factors that can enter into play during decision making processes. For example, while many types of biases exist, the actor-observer bias (also known as the actor-observer asymmetry) is particularly salient when considering perception and posture towards other people (see, e.g., Nadelhoffer and Feltz, 2008). This type of bias manifests when an individual believes their own actions are governed by external forces (e.g., situational rather than personality), while other peoples' behavior is governed by internal forces (e.g., personality rather than situational; Malle, 2006). This can manifest when a decision maker (e.g., a purchasing officer) responsible to awarding contracts discovers modern slavery at a supplier location, attributing the incident to forces outside their control; however, they may in turn blame the supplier directly for the infraction regardless of the level of control the supplier had directly over the situation. This shares similarities as well with positivity bias, where individuals will blame 'external forces' when there are negative consequences associated with their actions.

5.3.6   Other Cognitive Factors

There are other cognitive factors as well that may influence modern slavery-related decisions in global supply chains. For example, moral dissonance is when one's behavior or actions are in conflict with their beliefs (Lowell, 2012); this could occur when decision makers are faced with instances of modern slavery at supply locations and have to choose how to manage or approach the issue moving forward—knowing that their compensation may be at stake. Confirmation bias is the tendency for individuals to recall, interpret, or actively search for information which supports their point of view, values, or beliefs (Klayman, 1995). Purchasing managers, for example, who claim that modern slavery does not exist in their supply chains because they simply 'have not found anything' are likely facing this bias under logical fallacy. Self-serving bias operates alongside moral disengagement and ethical fading in that 'negative' events, such as modern slavery, are associated with outside or uncontrollable factors (Shepperd et al., 2008). An individual experiencing this bias could simultaneously be morally disengaging or ethically fading as they 'displace' blame for events elsewhere.

5.4   ORGANIZATIONAL AND SITUATIONAL FACTORS

5.4.1   Culture (organizational)

Organizational culture is perhaps one of the most important elements affecting (un)ethical decision making of employees (Zaal et al., 2019). In this regard, a number of theoretical frameworks can be considered to investigate the impact of culture on modern slavery studies in supply chains. First, ethical decision-making theory (Rest, 1986; 1994) envisages four psychological processes including recognition of a moral issue, formation of a moral judgment, establishment of moral intent, and the follow through on the intent to make an ethical decision. The lack of an ethical organizational culture can trigger any of the four psychological processes leading into unethical behavior. Especially with respect to modern slavery issues of suppliers, the formation of these four psychological processes by the buying firm and factors affecting these processes can be studied. Second, moral foundations theory (Graham et al., 2013) proposes five foundations (care vs. harm, fairness vs. cheating, authority vs. subversion, loyalty vs. betrayal, and sanctity vs. degradation) that form human morality. Assessing the value that organizational culture puts on any of these foundations and their impact on decisions toward modern slavery cases in supply chains can be a valuable potential direction for future research.

5.4.2   Power (organizational)

There is no denying that being in a position of power can significantly increase (un)ethical behavior in any given setting. For instance, if a head of procurement prioritizes cost savings over the well-being of their suppliers' employees, this can increasingly make weaker suppliers prone to modern slavery type conditions. Wal-Mart, as an example here, has been scrutinized for decades regarding labor violations throughout their supply chain. More recently, violations surfaced pertaining to mistreatment of women in the garment supply chain (Bhattacharjee, 2019). Given Wal-Mart's position as a global retail giant, lead procurement officers and executive buyers hold tremendous power. In addition, subordinate employees within the buying firm will likely also align with the head of procurement's decision making. Yet, a quite insightful line of research would be on how these subordinates, assumingly in lower positions of power, can resist such decisions and instead make a positive impact towards ethical decision making (Cremer and Moore, 2020). Social learning theory (Brown et al., 2005) explores how individuals learn by paying attention to others' behaviors, attitudes, and values. The learning is not only confined to subordinates learning from leaders but also leaders learning from their subordinates (Desai and Kouchaki, 2017).

5.4.3 Time Pressure (situational)

If the weight of stress was not enough in this world, mix in time pressure to further exacerbate the issue. While there are positive outcomes associated with certain levels of time pressure, too much or overwhelming pressures can lead to extreme narrowing of focus and anxiety, especially when greater uncertainty exists (Maule et al., 2000). Time pressure became a greater reality for many firms with Covid-19 stretching and extending re-supply and lead times. Under shorter, more stressful decision-making windows, many firms neglected their ESG-related commitments in order to bolster profiteering and survival (Ranjbari et al., 2021). From a modern slavery lens, this may be further exacerbated at supply locations where buyers are looking to get what they need quickly, overlooking the 'human' conditions present.

5.5 CONCLUSION

In this chapter we aimed at introducing the field of behavioral ethics to the study of modern slavery in supply chains through discussions surrounding cognitive, organizational, and situational factors. The intent behind introducing behavioral ethics to modern slavery literature in supply chains has been the main idea in this field, as people with good intentions are still capable of doing bad things. Extending this idea to the omnipresent cases of modern slavery in global supply chains, we explored several theories and frameworks in behavioral ethics that might be able to help explain why organizations remain complacent toward modern slavery. We handpicked and introduced some of these major frameworks and theories including but not limited to bounded awareness and bounded ethicality, social cognitive theory or moral disengagement, neutralization, ethical fading, and a range of various other factors considered to be 'cognitive factors.' We also explored culture and power as 'organizational factors' as well as actor-observer bias and time pressure as 'situational factors' that might help to explain complacency toward modern slavery. We however would like to emphasize that this attempt only provides a brief overview of a quite broad and fast-growing field varying across topics and methodologies.

With respect to methodologies, fundamentally behavioral studies are associated with conducing controlled lab experiments (Fahimnia et al., 2019). Having said that, data triangulations and using a combination of field data and lab experiments are the new promising frontiers in conducting behavioral ethics studies (Cremer and Moore, 2020). In order to get a thorough understanding of how managers 'sensitize' themselves to modern slavery, it is imperative that we broaden our methodological toolkit. In our view, it is important that we digress from the traditional (and widely accepted) methodological techniques. For example, we need to move beyond positivist case studies. It will be very insightful conducting ethnographic research (Zilber and Zanoni, 2022) where scholars can embed themselves in the field for a longer duration. This will facilitate understanding the cultural nuances of how and why people get trapped in such situations. This may involve conducing field research in the cotton fields of Pakistan or Uzbekistan if, for example, one was investigating the fashion industry. We also see merit in longitudinal processual studies (Langley, 1999) where changes can be observed over time, whether the living conditions of victims have improved, and how they have reskilled themselves to re-enter the work force. In addition, with the disclosure-based legislations gaining currency and numerous modern slavery reports being analyzed, it will be important to gauge whether reporting of modern slavery incidents leads to change of behavior and influences reporting for other organizations in similar industries. Discourse analysis (Hardy et al., 2020) would be a useful methodology to employ as we may be able to see how internal policy changes are being enacted. Finally, for data collection, we may need more creative leveraging of videos and photographs (Jarrett and Liu, 2016; LeBaron et al., 2017) and also apply more innovative methods for analysis, moving beyond standard templates (Köhler et al., 2022) in qualitative research.

REFERENCES

Amnesty International (2021). Italy – a slippery slope for human rights: The Iuventa case. https:// www .amnesty .org/ en/ wp -content/ uploads/ 2021/ 08/ EUR3044752021ENGLISH.pdf

Ariely, D., & Jones, S. (2012). *The (honest) truth about dishonesty*. Harper Collins Publishers.

Bandura, A. (1986). *Social foundations of thought and action*. Prentice Hall.

Bandura, A. (1991). Social cognitive theory of self-regulation. *Organizational Behavior and Human Decision Processes*, 50(2), 248-287.

Bandura, A. (1999). Moral disengagement in the perpetration of inhumanities. *Personality and Social Psychology Review*, 3(3), 193-209.

Bazerman, M. (2014). *The power of noticing: What the best leaders see*. Simon and Schuster.

Bazerman, M., & Moore, D.A. (2012). Judgment in managerial decision making (8th ed.). Wiley & Sons.

Bazerman, M.H., & Banaji, M.R. (2004). The social psychology of ordinary ethical failures. *Social Justice Research*, 17, 111-115.

Bazerman, M.H., & Chugh, D. (2006). Decisions without blinders. *Harvard Business Review*, 84(1), 88.

Bazerman, M.H., & Gino, F. (2012). Behavioral ethics: Toward a deeper understanding of moral judgment and dishonesty. *Annual Review of Law and Social Science*, 8(1), 85-104.

Bazerman, M.H., & Sezer, O. (2016). Bounded awareness: Implications for ethical decision making. *Organizational Behavior and Human Decision Processes*, 136, 95-105.

Bendoly, E., Croson, R., Goncalves, P., & Schultz, K. (2010). Bodies of knowledge for research in behavioral operations. *Production and Operations Management*, 19(4), 434-452.

Benstead, A.V., Hendry, L.C., & Stevenson, M. (2021). Detecting and remediating modern slavery in supply chains: A targeted audit approach. *Production Planning & Control*, 32(13), 1136-1157.

Bhattacharjee, S.S. (2019). Fast fashion, production targets, and gender-based violence in Asian garment supply chains. In: Saxena, S. (ed.), *Labor, Global Supply Chains, and the Garment Industry in South Asia: Bangladesh after Rana Plaza*, Routledge, 207-227.

Brown, M.E., Treviño, L.K., & Harrison, D.A. (2005). Ethical leadership: A social learning perspective for construct development and testing. *Organizational Behavior and Human Decision Processes*, 97(2), 117-134.

Caruana, R., Crane, A., Gold, S., & LeBaron, G. (2021). Modern slavery in business: The sad and sorry state of a non-field. *Business & Society*, 60(2), 251-287.

Chan, E. (2021). It has been 8 years since the Rana Plaza disaster. What's changed? *VOGUE*. https://www.vogue.co.uk/news/article/rana-plaza-disaster-8-years

Chugh, D., & Bazerman, M.H. (2007). Bounded awareness: What you fail to see can hurt you. *Mind & Society*, 6(1), 1-18.

Chugh, D., Bazerman, M.H., & Banaji, M.R. (2005). Bounded ethicality as a psychological barrier to recognizing conflicts of interest. Conflicts of interest: Challenges and solutions. *Business, Law, Medicine, and Public Policy*, 17(1), 74-95.

Cremer, D.D., & Moore, C. (2020). Toward a better understanding of behavioral ethics in the workplace. *Annual Review of Organizational Psychology and Organizational Behavior*, 7(1), 369-393.

De Cremer, D., Mayer, D.M., & Schminke, M. (2010a). Guest editors' introduction: On understanding ethical behavior and decision making: A behavioral ethics approach. *Business Ethics Quarterly*, 20(1), 1-6.

De Cremer, D., & Tenbrunsel, A.E. (2012). *Behavioral business ethics: Shaping an emerging field*. Taylor & Francis.

De Cremer, D., Tenbrunsel, A.E., & van Dijke, M. (2010b). Regulating ethical failures: Insights from psychology. *Journal of Business Ethics*, 95(1), 1-6.

De Cremer, D., & Vandekerckhove, W. (2017). Managing unethical behavior in organizations: The need for a behavioral business ethics approach. *Journal of Management & Organization*, 23(3), 437-455.

Desai, S.D., & Kouchaki, M. (2017). Moral symbols: A necklace of garlic against unethical requests. *Academy of Management Journal*, 60(1), 7-28.

Fahimnia, B., Pournader, M., Siemsen, E., Bendoly, E., & Wang, C. (2019). Behavioral operations and supply chain management–a review and literature mapping. *Decision Sciences*, 50(6), 1127-1183.

Gerlach, P., Teodorescu, K., & Hertwig, R. (2019). The truth about lies: A meta-analysis on dishonest behavior. *Psychological Bulletin*, 145(1), 1-44.

Graham, J., Haidt, J., Koleva, S., Motyl, M., Iyer, R., Wojcik, S.P., & Ditto, P.H. (2013). Chapter two - moral foundations theory: The pragmatic validity of moral pluralism. *Advances in Experimental Social Psychology*, 47, 55-130.

Hardy, C., Bhakoo, V., & Maguire, S. (2020). A new methodology for supply chain management: Discourse analysis and its potential for theoretical advancement. *Journal of Supply Chain Management*, 56(2), 19-35.

Jarrett, M., & Liu, F. (2016). 'Zooming with': A participatory approach to the use of video ethnography in organizational studies. *Organizational Research Methods*, 21(2), 366-385.

Klayman, J. (1995). Varieties of confirmation bias. *Psychology of Learning and Motivation*, 32, 385-418.

Klockars, C.B. (1974). *The professional fence*. Free Press.

Köhler, T., Smith, A., & Bhakoo, V. (2022). Templates in qualitative research methods: Origins, limitations, and new directions. *Organizational Research Methods*, 25(2), 183-210.

Langley, A. (1999). Strategies for theorizing from process data. *Academy of Management Review*, 24(4), 691-710.

LeBaron, C., Jarzabkowski, P., Pratt, M.G., & Fetzer, G. (2017). An introduction to video methods in organizational research. *Organizational Research Methods*, 21(2), 239-260.

Loewenstein, G. (1996). Behavioral decision theory and business ethics: Skewed tradeoffs between self and other. In: Messick, D.M., & Tenbrunsel, A.E. (eds.), *Codes of conduct: Behavioral Research into Business Ethics*, Russell Sage Foundation, 214-227.

Lowell, J. (2012). Managers and moral dissonance: Self justification as a big threat to ethical management? *Journal of Business Ethics*, 105(1), 17-25.

Malle, B.F. (2006). The actor-observer asymmetry in attribution: A (surprising) meta-analysis. *Psychological Bulletin*, 132(6), 895.

Matza, D. (2018). *Delinquency and drift*. Routledge.

Maule, A.J., Hockey, G.R.J., & Bdzola, L. (2000). Effects of time-pressure on decision-making under uncertainty: Changes in affective state and information processing strategy. *Acta Psychologica*, 104(3), 283-301.

Meshram, K., Bhakoo, V., & Bove, L.L. (2021). Building and sustaining an anti-slavery business model: A tale of two fashion brands. *Journal of Strategic Marketing*, 1-27.

Minor, W.W. (1980). The neutralization of criminal offense. *Criminology*, 18(1), 103-120.

Moore, C., & Gino, F. (2015). Approach, ability, aftermath: A psychological process framework of unethical behavior at work. *Academy of Management Annals*, 9(1), 235-289.

Nadelhoffer, T., & Feltz, A. (2008). The actor–observer bias and moral intuitions: Adding fuel to sinnott-armstrong's fire. *Neuroethics*, 1(2), 133-144.

Nieuwenboer, N.A.D., Cunha, J.V.D., & Treviño, L.K. (2017). Middle managers and corruptive routine translation: The social production of deceptive performance. *Organization Science*, 28(5), 781-803.

Nolan, J., & Boersma, M. (2019). *Addressing modern slavery*. UNSW Press.

Polding, B. (2017). The extension of neutralization theory to business ethics. *Journal of Leadership Studies*, 11(2), 63-65.

Ranjbari, M., Shams Esfandabadi, Z., Zanetti, M.C., Scagnelli, S.D., Siebers, P.-O., Aghbashlo, M., . . . & Tabatabaei, M. (2021). Three pillars of sustainability in the wake of covid-19: A systematic review and future research agenda for sustainable development. *Journal of Cleaner Production*, 297, 126660.

Rees, M.R., Tenbrunsel, A.E., & Bazerman, M.H. (2019). Bounded ethicality and ethical fading in negotiations: Understanding unintended unethical behavior. *Academy of Management Perspectives*, 33(1), 26-42.

Rest, J.R. (1986). *Moral development: Advances in research and theory*. Praeger.

Rest, J.R. (1994). Background: Theory and research. In: Rest, J.R., & Narvaez, D. (eds.), *Moral development in the professions*, Lawrence Erlbaum Associates, 1-26.

Schminke, M., Caldwell, J., Ambrose, M.L., & McMahon, S.R. (2014). Better than ever? Employee reactions to ethical failures in organizations, and the ethical recovery paradox. *Organizational Behavior and Human Decision Processes*, 123(2), 206-219.

Shepperd, J., Malone, W., & Sweeny, K. (2008). Exploring causes of the self-serving bias. *Social and Personality Psychology Compass*, 2(2), 895-908.

Simons, D.J., & Chabris, C.F. (1999). Gorillas in our midst: Sustained inattentional blindness for dynamic events. *Perception*, 28(9), 1059-1074.

Simpson, D., Segrave, M., Quarshie, A., Kach, A., Handfield, R., Panas, G., & Moore, H. (2021). The role of psychological distance in organizational responses to modern slavery risk in supply chains. *Journal of Operations Management*, 67(8), 989-1016.

Tenbrunsel, A., & Smith-Crowe, K. (2008). Ethical decision making: Where we've been and where we're going. *The Academy of Management Annals*, 2(1), 545-607.

Tenbrunsel, A.E., Diekmann, K.A., Wade-Benzoni, K.A., & Bazerman, M.H. (2010). The ethical mirage: A temporal explanation as to why we are not as ethical as we think we are. *Research in Organizational Behavior*, 30, 153-173.

Tenbrunsel, A.E., & Messick, D.M. (2004). Ethical fading: The role of self-deception in unethical behavior. *Social Justice Research*, 17(2), 223-236.

Trautrims, A., Gold, S., Touboulic, A., Emberson, C., & Carter, H. (2021). The UK construction and facilities management sector's response to the modern slavery act: An intra-industry initiative against modern slavery. *Business Strategy & Development*, 4(3), 279-293.

Trevino, L.K., & Weaver, G.R. (1994). Business ethics/business ethics: One field or two? *Business Ethics Quarterly*, 4(2), 113-128.

Treviño, L.K., Weaver, G.R., & Reynolds, S.J. (2006). Behavioral ethics in organizations: A review. *Journal of Management*, 32(6), 951-990.

Villena, V.H., Wilhelm, M., & Xiao, C.Y. (2021). Untangling drivers for supplier environmental and social responsibility: An investigation in Philips Lighting's Chinese supply chain. *Journal of Operations Management*, 67(4), 476-510.

Wilhelm, M., Kadfak, A., Bhakoo, V., & Skattang, K. (2020). Private governance of human and labor rights in seafood supply chains – the case of the modern slavery crisis in Thailand. *Marine Policy*, 115, 103833.

Yawar, S.A., & Seuring, S. (2017). Management of social issues in supply chains: A literature review exploring social issues, actions and performance outcomes. *Journal of Business Ethics*, 141(3), 621-643.

Zaal, R.O.S., Jeurissen, R.J.M., & Groenland, E.A.G. (2019). Organizational architecture, ethical culture, and perceived unethical behavior towards customers: Evidence from wholesale banking. *Journal of Business Ethics*, 158(3), 825-848.

Zilber, T.B., & Zanoni, P. (2022). Templates of ethnographic writing in organization studies: Beyond the hegemony of the detective story. *Organizational Research Methods*, 25(2), 371-404.

6. Supply chain justice

Lee Matthews and Minelle E. Silva

Justice is the first virtue of social institutions, as truth is of systems of thought. A theory however elegant and economical must be rejected or revised if it is untrue; likewise laws and institutions no matter how efficient and well-arranged must be reformed or abolished if they are unjust.

John Rawls
Author of 'A theory of justice' and 'Justice as fairness'

6.1 IS SUPPLY CHAIN SUSTAINABILITY AN EFFICIENCY PROBLEM?

To start our chapter, we would like to engage in a thought experiment. Imagine a supply chain, for example, a global commodity supply chain for a product such as beef. Let us say that the cattle within this long supply chain are farmed in Brazil and sold by multinational corporations to retailers in the United States and Europe. Take a few minutes to imagine all the stakeholders there are for such a supply chain. Besides the obvious candidates (customers, investors, governments, etc.), there may be Indigenous peoples whose land rights have been, or are threatened with being, violated (Amnesty International, 2020), there may be workers working in conditions of modern slavery (Emberson, 2019), and human rights defenders who are concerned about the effects this supply chain has on stakeholders' political, economic, social and environmental rights (OHCHR, 2022).

Now imagine that you are one of the stakeholders for this supply chain, but, somehow, you do not know which one. You could be the owner of a farm or an exploited worker on it, you could be an environmental defender threatened with physical violence (even murder) or one of the people making such threats against environmental defenders (Global Witness, 2022a). How would this supply chain look to you from behind this 'veil of ignorance' (Rawls, 2005)? What changes would you make to the organisation of this supply chain if there was a chance you could be one of the people worst impacted by it? Would you be concerned with the efficiency of the supply chain, how quickly and cheaply the beef can be sold in US and European markets? Or would you be more concerned with questions of justice? Would you want to ensure that human rights were respected in lines with the United Nations' (2011) 'Guiding Principles on Business and Human Rights'? Would you want to ensure that any past violations of land rights, and human rights generally, would be remedied by relevant governments and businesses? Would you want the distribution of economic value within the supply chain to be fair and equitable?

No doubt your answers to the questions posed by our thought experiment would be more concerned with justice than efficiency, which begs the very important question: Should justice, rather than efficiency, be the dominant logic for the organisation of global supply chains?

In our thought experiment, it should be noted that there is a distinction between efficiency and justice. While efficiency is based on customer-centred value, for instance, lower cost and improved quality, justice should consider people and fairness as central to guiding supply chain decisions. The distinction between efficiency and justice was originally made by the supply chain scholar Stephen New (1997). We believe that this distinction was ahead of its time but we are also of the opinion that there is now a constituency of supply chain scholars concerned with sustainability that will be willing to adopt justice lenses for the study of sustainable supply chain management (SSCM). In the next section, we outline a vision of what New (1997) called the 'just' supply chain.

6.2 SUPPLY CHAIN JUSTICE: UNDERSTANDING SSCM AS A JUSTICE PROBLEM

In this chapter, we understand SSCM as a justice problem (i.e. the focus shifts from efficiency towards a shared responsibility among supply chain members to remove structural inequalities within supply chains to achieve fairness for all supply chain stakeholders; Young, 2006). This justice approach contrasts with 'socio-efficiency' approaches to sustainability based on palliative actions intended to reduce harm (Dyllick and Hockerts, 2002) and instrumental supply chain perspectives on sustainability that prioritise protecting businesses rather than those who have suffered adverse impacts on their human rights (Meehan and Pinnington, 2021). In this chapter we present the novel concept of supply chain justice, which is based on the triple bottom line (TBL) framework but reinvigorates and expands its original concerns with social and environmental justice (Elkington, 1997). It synthesises the TBL concept and the emergent concept of 'corporate social justice' (CSJ), defined as 'an ongoing commitment to achieve a vision of justice or equity in partnership with stakeholders' (Zheng, 2020).

In the rest of this section, we update New's (1997) work on justice with insights from 25 years of theory and practice. We define supply chain justice as the design and management of supply chains according to the principles of social, economic and environmental justice. However, we do not *a priori* define the relationships between the three justice concepts as this will depend on each scholar's understanding of those concepts. For some, there will be a hierarchy among the concepts, while for others, they will be nested one within the other. Further, for those using supply chain justice as a lens for SSCM research, the relationship between the three justice concepts will also need to be determined empirically on a case-by-case basis, depending on the justice issues of a given supply chain and the (possibly conflicting) stakeholder perspectives on justice. Each of the three dimensions of supply chain justice will be looked at in the remainder of this section.

6.2.1   Economic Justice

Economic justice is concerned with fairness within political-economic systems, with the basic principle being egalitarianism (Rawls, 2001). Rawls (2001, 2005) states that economic development should be concerned with the welfare of the least advantaged in society. An economic action is therefore just if it can be said to increase the welfare of the least well off. At first glance, this seems to be consistent with socio-efficiency approaches to CSR and corporate sustainability in which businesses commit to minimum and living wages for workers in their supply chains and/or guarantee premium prices for commodity suppliers (Young, 2006). However, Rawls's (2001, 2005) rule goes much further than this. *Every* decision made in terms of designing and managing supply chains would need to consider the welfare of the least well off within the supply chain. Any business that adopted this rule for the management of the supply chain would need to radically reconceive what is meant by SSCM.

We also believe that economic justice needs to become central to SSCM as many 'companies play a role in creating and maintaining inequities through their supply chains' (Zheng, 2020), a fact that has long been recognised by scholars of Global Value Chains (GVCs) (Aguiar de Medeiros and Trebat, 2017) and NGOs concerned with questions of social justice (Peng et al., 2022). Often, there is an unacknowledged postcolonial legacy behind the unjust economic relations that characterise many global supply chains. This legacy is well put in the following quotation from the NGO Global Witness (2022b):

> The wealth of European and North American economies was created in large part by extracting land, resources and manpower from countries in Africa, South America and Asia, creating the vast economic inequality which so defines the world today. Even after formal decolonisation, this extractive economic model is maintained by powerful companies whose supply chains stretch across borders, showing little respect for either local communities or the environment.

Unless SSCM scholars want to be complicit in this 'extractive economic model', such postcolonial economic structures, and the ideologies that help perpetuate them, need to become a central concern for SSCM scholarship and the concept of supply chain justice can contribute towards this. Using justice lenses forces us to confront an awful reality hidden by the 'sustainability' strategies of multinational corporations: Global supply chains are not only scarred by multiple injustices but are also drivers of injustice themselves (Walker, 2019), through environmental destruction (Global Witness, 2022b), and adverse impacts on human rights (Butt et al., 2020). But scholars using the supply chain justice concept can also take inspiration from decolonized perspectives. For instance, Marques et al. (2021) claim that alternative concepts and epistemologies (e.g. Buen Vivir in Latin America) should be used to guide the production of sustainability knowledge, which can lead to the development of new business models based on decolonized approaches to organizing supply chains.

6.2.2 Social Justice

Social justice is a difficult concept to define as there are a bewildering number of conflicting frameworks and interpretations. For example, the International Forum for Social Development (2006, p. 7), a three-year project conducted by United Nations' Department of Economic and Social Affairs, defines social justice 'broadly' as 'the fair and compassionate distribution of the fruits of economic growth'. However, others see economic growth and social justice as antithetical, for example those in the 'degrowth' movement (Escobar, 2015). Reflecting the difficulty of working with the social justice concept, Ornstein (2017) identified 30 'basic' principles of social justice. Despite the complexity of the discourse on social justice, there is, nevertheless, an overarching principle, which is that fairness and compassion should be basis of all social systems (Rawls, 2001, 2005).

Social justice was one of the three bottom lines presented in Elkington's (1997) TBL framework, along with 'economic prosperity' and 'environmental quality'. The adoption of the TBL framework as the basis for the study of SSCM provided an opportunity, as yet largely untaken, to make the concept of justice central to the study of supply chain scholarship. The emergence of SSCM scholarship on 'social sustainability' presents an opportunity to reconceive 'social performance' in terms of social justice but, to date, social justice is a term rarely used by supply chain scholars researching 'social sustainability'.

So how would a social justice perspective differ from a socio-efficiency perspective on 'social sustainability'? We will consider this in relation to Fair Trade (2022), an initiative to stimulate better prices and decent working conditions for farmers and workers in 'developing' economies. Fair Trade is a socio-efficiency strategy that reduces the social and economic harms caused by globalisation. However, while such harm reductions will undoubtedly benefit some farmers and workers (Hannibal and Kauppi, 2019), from a social justice perspective, other issues need to be considered. Young (2006) claims that where there are structural injustices, there will also be privileges. Those able to participate in Fair Trade can be seen as privileged compared to those too poor to join cooperatives (Mancini, 2013). Such socio-efficiency strategies, rather than benefitting the least advantaged may be reinforcing structural inequalities and be a source of exclusion for the poorest farmers and workers. This has implications for SSCM strategies, such as third-party assessment (Hannibal and Kauppi, 2019). Rather than simply assessing existing suppliers, social justice strategies may need to also consider who is excluded from the supply chain and develop action plans for their inclusion.

6.2.3   Environmental Justice

Environmental justice is an umbrella term to capture a wide variety of social movements fighting the injustices caused by the worsening environmental crisis. Elkington (1997) was concerned with environmental justice, which he saw as occurring at the intersection of the social justice and environmental quality bottom lines. But as with social justice, environmental justice has yet to become a significant area of research within SSCM scholarship.

Perhaps the most prominent justice movement at the moment is the 'climate justice' movement. For many decades, climate change was framed by scientific discourses but with the reality of anthropogenic global warming largely accepted nowadays, the focus has shifted to issues of fairness, the proper domain of the theory and practice of justice (Rawls, 2001). Is it fair that those least responsible for the climate crisis, the world's poor, are going to be most impacted by it? Returning to our earlier thought experiment, we can see that consumers in the United States and Europe are contributing to the climate crisis through the consumption of beef, which is a driver of deforestation and whose long global supply chains emit more carbon dioxide than would be emitted from alternative local supply chains (although other emissions will also affect local communities; see Chamanara et al., 2021). If we return to our list of stakeholders, the consumers in the US and Europe will have greater resources – power and privileges, according to Young (2006) – for mitigating the worst impacts of climate change than those indigenous peoples that have been evicted from their land or those working in conditions of modern slavery. Unfairly, due to the greater accumulated wealth of the United States and Europe, itself a consequence of colonialism and postcolonial exploitation, consumers in these countries will be less impacted by the climate crisis than those in the Global South (IPCC, 2022).

Climate justice also seeks to ensure that the solutions to the climate crisis are just. For example, carbon offsetting is becoming an increasingly common business practice but can have potential justice issues. This can be seen in the recent controversy in which Brew Dog, a UK brewer, was attempting to offset its supply chain emissions by reforesting land in Scotland. Allegedly, this initiative had the unintended consequence of pricing local people out of owning local land and property (Guardian, 2022). Climate justice is also believed to be a more effective concept for mobilising action on climate change as justice resonates more with people than scientific narratives. The logic of this argument is that the science induces despair, while the adoption of a justice lens will inspire action.

Climate justice can be considered a distinct form of justice or as part of the broader concept of environmental justice. The term environmental justice emerged as the name for a movement established in the US in the 1970s that fought environmental racism, a form of racism in which ethnic groups disproportionately suffer the worst environmental harms. In the subsequent decades it has evolved into an umbrella concept that covers a wide variety of responses to the worsening environmental crisis. Environmental justice has been called the 'environmentalism of the poor' and 'working-class environmentalism' and there are links with ecofeminism (Martinez-Alier et al., 2014). As well as climate justice, its concerns have expanded to 'ecological debt', 'biopiracy', 'water justice', 'the defence of the commons', 'biomass conflicts', 'territorial rights', 'toxic colonialism', 'transport justice' and 'food deserts'. It should be noted that environmental racism cuts across all of these issues, with ethnic groups and peoples of the Global South still suffering disproportionately from these multiple and overlapping injustices. Despite this, environmental racism has yet to emerge as a major concern within SSCM scholarship.

6.3   CONCLUSION AND FUTURE DIRECTIONS

The sustainability agenda that has guided business practice for the last 25 years is in crisis. There is a growing recognition that corporate sustainability has not been able to effect radical system change within social and natural systems at the pace and scale required (Elkington, 2018; Ergene, Banerjee and Hoffman, 2020; Gladwin, 2012). One of the most dramatic moments in this crisis came in 2018 when Elkington (2018) 'recalled' his TBL concept due to a lack of real-world progress on sustainability and a failure to stimulate a transformation in the nature of global capitalism.

One possible diagnosis for this crisis in the sustainability agenda that is relevant for SSCM scholarship is that sustainability performance has traditionally been framed as an efficiency problem rather than a question of justice (Ehrenfeld, 2005). This efficiency perspective has led to the TBL failing to achieve its potential for 'systemic change' (Elkington, 2018). In this chapter, we present justice as an alternative to the efficiency paradigm. By reframing TBL through justice lens, we showed that responsibility should be shared among supply chain stakeholders, taking in consideration the ways in which the different statuses, power and privileges of supply chain members affects the organisation of global supply chains (Young, 2006). Therefore, more than a new oxymoron, supply chain justice should emerge as an alternative theorization of SSCM where social, environmental and economic justice are embedded in the supply chain structure.

Clearly, justice is emerging as an increasingly central concept within the discourse on sustainability and in other academic fields (e.g. Human Geography and Political Ecology); justice lenses are also increasingly used in the study of global value chains. SSCM scholarship is out of step with these trends, however. This, in itself, is a significant issue that needs to be addressed, but there is also a more significant issue: many global supply chains are structured according to, and reinforce, exploitative postcolonial economic relations between the North and South and West and East. Eschewing socio-efficiency in favour of supply chain justice approaches should allow for the emergence of alternative ways of organisation that can help supply chain stakeholders to escape the iron cage of instrumental rationality (Gold and Schleper, 2017). This can encourage the emergence of new business models based on alternative ways of thinking (e.g. Buen Vivir in Latin America; Giovannini, 2012), although more research on these possibilities is needed. Further studies should understand the contribution of social business and other alternative business forms (e.g. Benefit Corporations [US] and B-Corp certified businesses) to the realisation of supply chain justice. In addition, it would be useful to explore whether non-traditional businesses are better able than transnational corporations to overcome the power imbalances within globalised political-economic structures to drive justice outcomes within their supply chains.

We also hope that the concept of supply chain justice will be useful for 'activist' approaches towards SSCM. Just as climate justice inspires people to act against the injustices posed by Anthropogenic Global Warming, we hope that supply chain justice will inspire SSCM scholars to become activist researchers (Touboulic and McCarthy, 2020) and/or engage in Critical Engaged Research (Touboulic et al., 2020). Such a perspective is not limited to how they conduct research or engage with specific theories, but to which voices they represent regarding different (political) spaces, such as those on the periphery of the globalised economy (Dussel, 2003). Pursuing supply chain justice is a mean of expressing a political interpretation of responsibility (cf. Young, 2006).

While we believe there are a number of significant advantages to adopting justice as a lens for SSCM scholarship, it would be remiss of us not to acknowledge some of the issues that supply chain scholars may have adopting justice lenses. The first issue is that justice is, like concepts such as democracy and sustainability, an 'essential contested concept' (Gallie, 1956) – in other words, a concept that will never be defined in a way that will be universally agreed upon. But the status of justice as an essentially contested concept is only a problem if we are not willing to clearly state the definition of justice we are using, or the assumptions upon which it is based, and are unwilling to enter into dialogue with those who have used a different definition and have different assumptions about justice.

There is also a specific issue for academics using the concept of environmental justice, which is that this concept and its large vocabulary were developed not by academics but by activists within the environmental justice movement. SSCM scholars will need to be comfortable working with these 'grassroots' concepts and need to be careful not to be seen by environmental justice activists to be appropriating the discourse of their movement for our own instrumental purposes as academics (e.g. publication for career development; Martinez-Alier et al., 2014). Adopting an activist position as SSCM scholars may also help us gain acceptance from this movement.

To conclude our chapter, we would like to return to the thought experiment with which we started the chapter. This thought experiment is based on Rawl's (2001, 2005) original thought experiment, the 'original position'. In this thought experiment, readers were asked to reflect on how society is organised from behind an imagined 'veil of ignorance' (i.e., they had to imagine that they did not know what position they occupied in society). From behind the 'veil of ignorance', they had to imagine how society should be organised. Would they believe that society should be organised in the same way if there were a possibility they were among the least advantaged? We believe our adaptation of this thought experiment in which supply chain managers are invited to reflect upon the organisation of their supply chains from behind a 'veil of ignorance' may be a useful way to help them shift from the efficiency paradigm towards the justice paradigm. We hope this thought experiment will be of use to scholars trying to challenge the mental models of supply chain managers through activist and engaged scholarship.

REFERENCES

Aguiar de Medeiros, C., & Trebat, N. (2017). Inequality and income distribution in global value chains. *Journal of Economic Issues*, 51(2), 401-408.

Amnesty International (2020). Brazil: Cattle illegally grazed in the Amazon found in supply chain of leading meat-packer JBS. https://www.amnesty.org/en/latest/

news/2020/07/brazil-cattle-illegally-grazed-in-the-amazon-found-in-supply-chain-of-leading-meat-packer-jbs/

Butt, N., Lambrick, F., Menton, M., & Renwick, A. (2019). The supply chain of violence. *Nature Sustainability*, 2(8), 742-747.

Chamanara, S., Goldstein, B., & Newell, J. P. (2021). Where's the beef? Costco's meat supply chain and environmental justice in California. *Journal of Cleaner Production*, 278, 123744.

Dussel, E. (2003). *Philosophy of liberation*. Wipf and Stock Publishers.

Dyllick, T., & Hockerts, K. (2002). Beyond the business case for corporate sustainability. *Business Strategy and the Environment*, 11(2), 130-141.

Ehrenfeld, J.R. (2005). The roots of sustainability. *MIT Sloan Management Review*, 46(2), 23-25.

Elkington, J. (1997). *Cannibals with forks: The triple bottom line of the 21st century*. Capstone.

Elkington, J. (2018). 25 years ago I coined the phrase 'triple bottom line.' Here's why it's time to rethink it. *Harvard Business Review*, 25, 2-5.

Emberson, C. (2019). Tackling slavery in supply chains: lessons from Brazilian-UK beef and timber. https://www.nottingham.ac.uk/research/beacons-of-excellence/rights-lab/resources/reports-and-briefings/2019/march/tackling-slavery-in-supply-chains.pdf

Ergene, S., Banerjee, S.B., & Hoffman, A.J. (2021). (Un)sustainability and organization studies: Towards a radical engagement. *Organization Studies*, 42(8), 1319-1335.

Escobar, A. (2015). Degrowth, postdevelopment, and transitions: a preliminary conversation. *Sustainability Science*, 10(3), 451-462.

Fair Trade (2022). What is Fair Trade? https://www.fairtrade.net/about/what-is-fairtrade

Gallie, W.B. (1956). Essentially contested concepts. *Proceedings of the Aristotelian Society*, 56, 167-198.

Giovannini, M. (2012). Social enterprises for development as Buen Vivir. *Journal of Enterprising Communities: People and Places in the Global Economy*, 6(3), 284-299.

Gladwin, T.N. (2012). Capitalism critique: Systemic limits on business harmony with nature. In: Bansal, P., Hoffman, A. (eds.), *The Oxford Handbook on Business and the Natural Environment*, Oxford University Press, 657-674.

Global Witness (2022a). Brazil. https://www.globalwitness.org/en/all-countries-and-regions/brazil/

Global Witness (2022b). What is climate justice? https://www.globalwitness.org/en/blog/what-climate-justice/

Gold, S., & Schleper, M.C. (2017). A pathway towards true sustainability: A recognition foundation of sustainable supply chain management. *European Management Journal*, 35(4), 425-429.

Guardian (2022). Lost Forest: Why is BrewDog's green scheme causing controversy? https://www.theguardian.com/environment/2022/mar/05/lost-forest-why-is-brewdog-green-scheme-causing-controversy

Hannibal, C., & Kauppi, K. (2019). Third party social sustainability assessment: is it a multi-tier supply chain solution? *International Journal of Production Economics*, 217, 78-87.

International Forum for Social Development (2006). Social justice in an open world: The role of the United Nations. https://www.un.org/esa/socdev/documents/ifsd/SocialJustice.pdf

IPCC (2022). Climate change 2022: Mitigation of Climate Change. https://www.ipcc .ch/report/sixth-assessment-report-working-group-3/

Mancini, M.C. (2013). Geographical indications in Latin America value chains: A 'branding from below' strategy or a mechanism excluding the poorest? *Journal of Rural Studies*, 32, 295-306.

Marques, L., Silva, M.E., & Matthews, L. (2021). Building the Latin American land-scape in supply chain sustainability research: How to break free from the hamster wheel? *Latin American Business Review*, 22(4), 309-321.

Martinez-Alier, J., Anguelovski, I., Bond, P., Del Bene, D., Demaria, F., Gerber, J.F., Greyl, L., Haas, W., Healy, H., Marín-Burgos, V., & Ojo, G. (2014). Between activism and science: grassroots concepts for sustainability coined by Environmental Justice Organizations. *Journal of Political Ecology*, 21(1), 19-60.

Meehan, J., & Pinnington, B.D. (2021). Modern slavery in supply chains: Insights through strategic ambiguity. *International Journal of Operations & Production Management*, 41(2), 77-101.

New, S.J. (1997). The scope of supply chain management research. *Supply Chain Management: An International Journal*, 2(1), 15-22.

OHCHR (2022). About human rights defenders. https:// www .ohchr .org/ en/ special -procedures/sr-human-rights-defenders/about-human-rights-defenders

Ornstein, A.C. (2017). Social justice: History, purpose and meaning. *Society*, 54(6), 541-548.

Peng, S., Jia, F., & Doherty, B. (2022). The role of NGOs in sustainable supply chain management: a social movement perspective. *Supply Chain Management: An International Journal*, 27(3), 383–408.

Rawls, J. (2001). *Justice as fairness* (2nd revised edition). Harvard University Press.

Rawls, J. (2005). *A theory of justice: Original edition*. Harvard University Press.

Touboulic, A., & McCarthy, L. (2020). Collective action in SCM: a call for activist research. *The International Journal of Logistics Management*, 31(1), 3-20.

Touboulic, A., McCarthy, L., & Matthews, L. (2020). Re-imagining supply chain challenges through critical engaged research. *Journal of Supply Chain Management*, 56(2), 36-51.

United Nations (2011). Guiding principles on business and human rights: Implementing the United Nations 'Protect, Respect and Remedy' Framework. New York and Geneva.

UN News (2021). Access to a healthy environment, declared a human right by UN rights council. https://news.un.org/en/story/2021/10/1102582

Walker, M.R. (2019). *Protecting the workforce: A defense of workers' rights in global supply chains*. Rowman & Littlefield.

Young, I.M. (2006). Responsibility and global justice: A social connection model. *Social Philosophy and Policy*, 23(1), 102-130.

Zheng, L. (2020). We're entering the age of Corporate Social Justice. https://hbr.org/ 2020/06/were-entering-the-age-of-corporate-social-justice

7. Wages, prices, and power: can customer-mandated living wages solve supply chain exploitation?

Steve New

7.1 INTRODUCTION

> Too many people are undervalued or excluded. Too many people don't earn a living wage. Too many people are held back through lack of skills. We aspire for a more equitable and inclusive world. And we have a plan to help create one.

Unilever tweet 21 January 2021[1]

The development of the global economy over the last forty years or so has seen remarkable increases in aggregate levels of standard of living, life expectancy and levels of education.[2] This success story is in many ways the story of supply chains: the remarkable systems of global industry which underpin contemporary prosperity. The proportion of international trade that involves global value chains is estimated to be 70% by the OECD[3]; the World Bank use a different methodology and arrive at a number just short of 50%.[4] In 2015, the ILO estimated that 20% of jobs were linked with global supply chains.[5] Within the UK, it is estimated that 14% of the UK workforce is employed just in the food and drink supply chain.[6] It is not fanciful to think of the emergence of 'supply chain capitalism' as one of the dominant motifs of the age (Tsing, 2009); the global value chain is 'the characteristic form of twenty-first-century global capitalism' (Nathan et al., 2022). Some writers use the phrase 'monopsony capitalism' (cheating slightly, to avoid the ugliness of the word 'oligopsony') to capture the idea that a key feature of this new world order is a small number of large multinational (buying) firms who exercise commercial power over much larger numbers of relatively weak suppliers (Kumar, 2020; Nathan et al., 2022). The story of economic transformation is also a story about the concentration of power.

Associated with these developments are serious concerns about the massively unequal distribution of costs and benefits; although supply chains have contributed to the 'Great Escape' from poverty (Deaton, 2013), a billion or so humans remain in extraordinary deprivation. Furthermore, the abundance of material goods and food for the wealthy seems somehow to come at the expense of many at the far end of the chain. There is a general sense that that Western/Northern affluence comes at too high a price (Lessenich, 2019; Purves, 2022). Supply chains, far from being devices for lifting people to riches, may instead act as shackles that confine the poor to relentless economic servitude. As rich consumers enjoy super-abundance, supply chains are rife with the worst forms of exploitation, including modern slavery.

Byanyima (2018), discussing research on supermarkets by the charity Oxfam, provides a crisp summary: big firms' supply chains drive poverty because 'brutal competition' leads them to exercise 'buying muscle' to 'squeeze their suppliers'. Selwyn (2019) discusses the phenomenon recasting 'value chains' as 'poverty chains': economically powerful companies drive down costs, which in turn drives down wages to exploitative levels. Campling and Quentin (2021) use the term 'global inequality chains'. At the individual level, this means that workers and their families suffer both immediate deprivation; they cannot accumulate either financial wealth or cultural capital (for example, being able to educate their children or participate effectively in civil society). At the level of firms, slender supplier profits prohibit investment, reducing the possibility of upgrading to more lucrative parts of the global value chain – an idea central to the body of work on 'global commodity chains' and 'global production networks' (Gereffi and Korzeniewicz, 1994; Coe, 2004). Nathan et al. (2022) characterise the situation in terms of a 'reverse subsidy': supplying firms, their workers, and – importantly – the workers' households and communities can be seen as providing a flow of wealth to the powerful buyers who control the chain, which is then passed on to affluent investors, grasping managers, and indulgent consumers.

At the macro level, this line of thinking aligns with 'Unequal Exchange Theory' (Emmanuel, 1972; Amin, 1976); the rich northern countries procure goods and commodities from poor southern ones at prices less than that which the provider nations can purchase them; this translates to a net resource transfer from the poor to the rich. In contrast to the Ricardian model of international trade working to mutual benefit, this model explicitly invokes the idea of relative power. Hickel et al. (2022) estimate that in this way, between 1990 and 2015, the global north appropriated resources and labour worth $242 trillion (in 2010 US$), equivalent to 25% of northern GDP.

Even within rich countries, recent years have delivered increased riches for the wealthy, and static or declining fortunes for the poorest. Contrary to traditional expectations, very high levels of employment have failed to translate into an improved financial position for the lowest-paid workers in advanced economies (Financial Times, 2019), with sharpening income inequality (Stone et al., 2020) and the emergence of 'in-work' poverty and exploitative working conditions. Across all countries, the least powerful in the supply chain continue to bear the brunt of disruptions such as the pandemic and war (Prapha, 2021).

As these outcomes have unfolded, a growing discourse has emerged focused on the morality of large companies – particularly the behemoths that sit astride complex global supply chains – under a variety of headings such as Responsible Capitalism, Corporate Social Responsibility (CSR), and Environmental, Social and Governance (ESG). This has crystallised into a bundle of approaches relating to how firms manage their supply base, the main tools being qualification (requiring suppliers to meet some criteria or other, such as ISO 14000, or to have a policy not to use child labour) and audit (where the buyer or some third party undertakes some check to see that a supplier's actions meet their claims). Setting minimum requirements for suppliers in codes of conduct is now established practice and can apply to many aspects of a supplier's business: in order for us to do business with you (says the buyer to the supplier), you must (for example) not employ children; not discriminate on grounds of gender; provide working conditions that must meet this particular industrial standard, and so on.

In this chapter, I will explore a case in which a major firm (Unilever) announces a policy to require a further—and very significant—condition: that its suppliers must pay their own workers no less than a specified (living) wage (Barrie, 2021). This is important for several reasons.

Firstly, as one of the world's largest consumer goods companies, Unilever wields considerable power. Like General Motors and IBM, it is an 'iconic' company whose scale, longevity and influence on consumers' lives makes it a significant element in the history of capitalism. Jones (2005, p. 7) comments that the firm 'provides a microcosm of many of the processes that have transformed the world', describing it as 'the global firm par excellence.' Its products are pervasive: according to Jones (2005), 50% of households in the world were making use of one or more of its extensive product lines (which span cleaning products, food and cosmetics). In a speech in 2014, CEO Paul Polman suggested the figure had become 70% (CGD, 2014). As a product company, it is one of a small number of firms that can stand up to the power of major retailers such as Wal-Mart and Tesco. Few other firms in the world could have the same impact on such a wide range of products and such numbers of consumers and suppliers. Few of Unilever's competing firms have made comparable commitments.[7]

Secondly, it appears to be a bold and radical step. The idea that suppliers might incur some (relatively marginal) extra costs to meet buyers' standards is not particularly controversial, particularly if end-consumers are happy to stump up a modest premium to ensure the products are 'green' or 'slavery-free'. The idea that buyers 'interfere' with their suppliers by demanding particular constraints on their operations is also well-established. But when suppliers' business models and competitiveness are fundamentally driven by labour costs, and when finding low prices is the DNA of corporate procurement, specifying the minimum wages payable to workers seems to cross a significant line. Although there are some precedents (principally in the textile industry), Unilever's approach is distinctive. Other 'commitments' to supply chain living wages have for the most part been made under the auspices of complex multi-stakeholder initiatives (and so potentially raising costs for the industry, not for a specific buying firm) and normally are framed as aspirations rather than hard rules (Edwards et al., 2019; LeBaron et al., 2022; Coneybear and Maguire, 2022). Unilever's stand has (on the face of it) significantly greater clarity and has a firm date for its implementation (2030).

Thirdly, the initiative has been widely hailed as an important step in addressing poverty in supply chains. It seems likely that if the plaudits and cheering are justified, Unilever's move may be a significant step forward in the progress of what might be framed as a new form of responsible capitalism. If it fails, or if it transpires to be merely an exercise of puffy public relations, it could provide a significant setback for those who champion 'enlightened capitalism' (Mayer, 2018; Mackey and Sisodia, 2014), and those see the application of commercial supply chain power as a key role in tackling the world's intersecting crises of climate and inequality (Humes, 2011).

The next section provides some necessary background to Unilever. I then go on to present a critique of the firm's promise, concluding by presenting three propositions to guide further research.

7.2   UNILEVER

Unilever has a complex UK-Dutch heritage, being formed by the merger in 1929 between Lever Brothers (the pioneer of branded soap) and Margarine Unie of the Netherlands (itself the result of mergers of other European food companies). The firm has a well-documented history, and it is relatively unusual for having opened its archives to serious historians rather than merely generating 'public relations' narratives. A two-volume history was produced by Cambridge University's Charles Wilson in 1954, followed up by a third volume in 1968; Harvard Business School's Geoffrey Jones picked up the story from the 1960s in 2005; other works include those by Fieldhouse (1978; 1994) and Reader (1980).

For most of its history, the firm has maintained an unusual dual nationality, with its leadership and headquarters operations split between the UK and the Netherlands. The only comparable company in this regard has been the oil giant Shell which, like Unilever, has now consolidated its position in the UK (Wilson, 2021; Nilsson and Khan, 2020).

An important feature of the firm is its vast range of products, including around four hundred brands in cleaning, personal care and food, including well-known labels such as Dove soap, Marmite spread and Cornetto ice creams[8]—brands between which consumers would not immediately draw connections. The name 'Unilever' was rarely found on products before 2004 and 2005, at which point the firm shifted towards a dualithic brand structure, enabling brands to be identified with both the specific brand identity and the parent company, the latter becoming increasingly significant in associations of corporate virtue, social responsibility, and sustainability (Brexendorf and Keller, 2017; Doyle et al., 2020; Raja, 2021). This presents a potential tension when the portfolio of brands is constantly shifting. During the period 2017 to 2021, the firm undertook 29 takeovers (€16bn) and 12 disposals (€11bn; Lex, 2022a): a brand acquired or disposed of suddenly gains or loses the aura of Unilever's corporate virtues. Additionally, the portfolio approach means that analysts and investors always have the possibility to see potential for restructuring; every component is potentially for sale, as investors seek synergies or focus in combining and separating lines of business. In 2017, the firm was a potential take-over target in a bid from food giant Kraft Heinz; in 2021, the firm sought (but repeatedly failed) to acquire the consumer products division of GSK (a 'fiasco'; Evans et al., 2022).

In recent years, the firm has become strongly identified with issues of CSR and sustainability, especially under the leadership of Polman, CEO from 2009 to 2018. In addition to the firm's extensive internal initiatives, it has been at the forefront of certain types of corporate political activism: it called for the ban of new petrol and diesel vehicles by 2035 (Miller and Campbell, 2022); it participated with other firms in the boycott of advertising on Facebook alongside the 'Stop Hate for Profit' campaign (Murphy, 2020). This has led to both praise and cynicism: 'the 21st century's poster child for corporate citizenship' (Corporate Knights, 2021); 'a company with a strong culture of integrity' (Henderson, 2022); 'no company embodies the marriage of wokeness and capitalism more than Unilever' (Ramaswamy, 2021, p. 41). Unilever is a leader among firms who have made environmental commitments (including a commitment to net zero emissions from all products by 2039[9] and halving its 2018 use of virgin plastic by 2025).[10]

Despite its ethical and progressive credentials, the firm has not been above criticism; it became embroiled in a complex dispute with one its businesses, Ben and Jerry's ice cream, over operations in the Palestinian Occupied Territories (Braithwaite, 2021; Wembridge, 2022). It has also faced long-standing controversies related to tea production in Kenya (Hervey, 2020; Schipani et al., 2022). Although it ceased exports and imports from Russia following the invasion of Ukraine in 2022, it continued to sell ice cream within the country after having declared it would only sell 'everyday essential foods'

(Evans, 2022b; Marlow, 2022). (In defence, Alan Jope, Polman's successor as CEO, commented that the economic contribution of this ongoing activity was trivial but that the decision was based on a commitment to the safety and well-being of the firm's Russian employees.)[11] Unilever is the world's biggest buyer of palm oil, which is a core ingredient in many of its businesses (including soap and ice cream), but which is associated with significant problems of deforestation and forced labour (Lex, 2022b).

The firm has also been accused of disingenuous marketing: for example, whereas Unilever maintained that 61% of its food and drink sales arose from products with 'High Nutritional Standards', an independent review arrived at a figure of 17%.[12] Unilever's climate targets were criticized as having 'very low integrity' and 'low transparency' in a report by the New Climate Institute and Carbon Market Watch (Day et al., 2022; Hook, 2022), following earlier criticisms about lack of transparency from the influential Climate Action 100+ investor group. The firm (alongside many of its peers) has been accused of lobbying against the introduction of deposit return schemes for plastic packaging (CMF 2022). It has also been accused of bad faith approaches to plastic packaging (Brock and Geddie, 2022): whilst publicly declaring their intention to eliminate plastic sachets (for products such as ketchup and shampoo), it is alleged that the firm lobbied for their retention (in India and the Philippines) and sought to wriggle around prohibitions on their sale (in Sri Lanka). The firm has also made misleading claims about the environmental merits of its products (Timmins, 2022). Other criticisms relate to the way in which its cosmetic advertising embodied potentially racist assumptions (i.e., white features are 'normal', while non-white ones are not; Evans, 2021b). It should be noted though, that on this and on other points, the firm has a history of listening to criticism (for example, in connection to the Living Wage—see below); on the use of stereotypes in advertising, the firm has changed its policies.[13]

These various assaults on Unilever's ethicality form part of a web of complex and interacting forces. For the champions of enlightened capitalism, the company is a beacon of hope. For others, the firm is seen as just another 'evil faceless corporation' (Craven-Matthews et al., 2021, p. 8) but with better public relations, and all the more dangerous for that. For conventional investors, the pursuit of ethicality is a distraction and an example of management hubris (Filippino et al., 2022). Well-known UK investors such as Terry Smith have claimed the firm has 'lost the plot' and has become 'obsessed with publicly displaying sustainability credentials'.[14] The famed activist investor Nelson Peltz joined the board of the company in May 2022 (Evans and Szalay, 2022), leading many to see increased pressure on the firms' leadership resulting in the announcement of Jope's departure in September 2022 (Jolly, 2022b). It is widely assumed that Peltz will also bring pressure for changes to the firm's ethical and sustainability commitments (Mundy et al., 2022). A significant review and reorganization of the business was already underway at the point of Peltz's arrival, leading to substantial job cuts (1,500, approximately 1% of the staff), and leaving the firm in 'defensive mode' (Lex, 2020c), poised to make substantial disposals of chunks of its business (Evans and Provan, 2022).

In this context, what should we make of Unilever's supply chain living wage promise? To understand this, it is worth exploring the background to the idea of minimum and living wages. State-mandated minimum wages emerged in many countries in the early part of the 20th century, often seen as a part of natural development to a more progressive and equitable society, a 'natural complement' to legislation governing safety in factories and public welfare (Webb and Webb, 1897; Snowden 1912). In the UK, minimum wages were initially established in 1909 in a handful of industrial sectors governed by 'Trade Boards' (later called Wages Councils; Fletcher, 2012). The political consensus allowed for this type of state interference in the market only under specific conditions: where labour lacked mobility, and where it was unable to organize into trades unions. Tennant (1909) describes how the antitoxin of a minimum wage should only be applied to the 'exceptionally unhealthy patches of the body politic...the morbid and diseased places...the industrial diphtheritic spots'.

Before long, idea of the minimum wage was being discussed as a universal right: Article 23 of the United Nations' Declaration of Human Rights (1948) states that workers are entitled to the right to 'just and favourable remuneration ensuring for himself and his family an existence worthy of human dignity, and supplemented, if necessary, by other means of social protection'.[15] As the century progressed, minimum wage policies were adopted across many countries, slowly encompassing more of the economy. Nearly all systems have intricate systems of exemptions and qualifications, and, driven by a fear of discouraging employment and economic growth, are often set at surprisingly low levels. Concern that minimum wages do not provide enough money to live on has led over the last 20 years or so to the emergence of the notion of the 'living wage', typically a higher threshold, assessed by civil society actors instead of government agencies (Dobbins and Prowse, 2021). Campaigning is then used to persuade organizations to go beyond the bare legal minimum requirements, often as part of a broader programme of corporate social responsibility and/ or reputation management. Although this development arose roughly in parallel across many countries, it is instructive to examine the case of the UK. In 2001—just a few years after the implementation of the official national minimum wage—an activist group began campaigning for a higher 'living wage', especially for workers in London where living costs were substantially higher than the rest of the country.[16] The campaign involved panels of experts arriving at independent judgements of the suitable level, and then pressurising companies to adopt commitments that they would (voluntarily) pay according to the model. In 2016, the UK Conservative Government then raised and relabelled the official minimum wage as 'the National Living Wage', a move that was derided by some commentators 'a remarkable act of political theatre' (Brown, 2017) as co-opting 'progressive language to cloak a regressive policy' (Butler, 2016) and 'stealing the clothes of anti-poverty campaigners' (Prentis, 2016).

Despite this and other linguistic subterfuges, the idea of the Living Wage in global supply chains has become a significant focus of various NGOs' (non-governmental organization) campaigning (Dobbins and Prowse, 2021), and recent years have seen a plethora of specific initiatives that have sought to rectify the 'Living Wage Gap'—construed variously as the difference a locally determined living wage between what workers typically earn, or the gap between the Living Wage and the prevailing legal minimum. NGOs and industry initiatives involved in this work include IDH (who operate multi-stakeholder initiative called the Roadmap on Living Wages—of which Unilever is a participant),[17] the Global Living Wage Coalition,[18] ACT (Action, Collaboration, Transformation),[19] the Asia Floor Wage Alliance,[20] the Clean Clothes Campaign,[21] and others. Broadly, these campaigns relate to industry-specific initiatives, focussing most notably on the textile and garment industry. The initiatives commonly reflect a position that 'efforts by individual companies to bring about wage improvements in individual supply chains—or in parts of them—have proven unlikely to be sustainable in the long run. It has become increasingly clear that the causes of low wages are systemic and therefore require systemic solutions' (Ergon Associates, 2015, p. 4).

In a critique of these developments, Edwards et al. (2019) enumerate several ways in which living wages initiatives in the garment industry have failed to live up to hopes. They note that outsourcing commitments to multi-stakeholder initiatives leads to painfully slow progress; they observe that progress is often hindered by debate about the technicalities of the calculation of the living wage, and that implementation is hindered by poor auditing and lack of transparency. They also observe that, although multi-stakeholder initiatives may include some participation by trades unions, the principle of freedom of association is often not enforced in practice.

In addition to these collective approaches, there are a relatively small number of organizations who have adopted individual initiatives regarding living wages in their supply base, but these have predominantly been associated with tightly defined programmes working in very specific commodities or domains (Dalmau, 2022); examples include Eosta, a fruit and vegetable producer who has introduced a living wage initiative in respect of mangoes,[22] the retail giant Tesco in respect of some banana suppliers,[23] and the defence engineering company BAe Systems, which has introduced a requirement for Living Wages for the contractors who work on BAe sites.[24] In contrast,

Unilever's supply chain Living Wage commitment appears to apply to all its suppliers, and so is worthy of more detailed scrutiny.

7.3   UNILEVER'S LIVING WAGE COMMITMENT

Unilever's policy is explained on the firm's website and in accompanying documents.[25] It sits in a rather confusing web of policies and initiatives: it forms part of the 'The Unilever Compass'[26] – a complex plan/infographic stating Unilever's purpose, which combines some rather oddly-phrased nostrums ('Brands with Purpose Grow'; 'Companies with Purpose Last'; 'People with Purpose Thrive'), grandiose goals ('Improve people's health, confidence and wellbeing') with more prosaic strategic objectives ('accelerate pure-play and omnichannel eCommerce'). This is complemented by a 34-page Responsible Sourcing Policy.[27] The announcement was made in January 2021:

> Ensuring that people earn a living wage or income is a critical step towards building a more equitable and inclusive society. It allows people to afford a decent standard of living, covering a family's basic needs: food, water, housing, education, healthcare, transportation, clothing; and includes a provision for unexpected events. A living wage should allow workers to participate fully in their communities and help them break the cycle of poverty.
>
> In addition, when people earn a living wage or income, there is a direct benefit to the economy, as it stimulates consumer spending, aids job creation, helps small businesses, decreases employee turnover and improves job productivity and quality – overall creating a virtuous cycle of economic growth.
>
> Our ambition is to improve living standards for low-paid workers worldwide. We will therefore ensure that everyone who directly provides goods and services to Unilever earns at least a living wage or income, by 2030. We already pay our employees at least a living wage, and we want to secure the same for more people beyond our workforce, specifically focusing on the most vulnerable workers in manufacturing and agriculture. We will work with our suppliers, other businesses, governments and NGOs – through purchasing practices, collaboration and advocacy – to create systemic change and global adoption of living wage practices.[28]

Everett (2021) quotes Unilever's Chief Procurement Officer Dave Ingram: 'It's not just giving families enough money to cover their basic needs plus a bit of a buffer, it also has clear, indirect benefits for the economy by stimulating spending and job creation, if it's done in the right way.' Jope explained the initiative would 'be a combination of encouragement in the beginning, auditing in the middle, and sanctioning towards the end. So by ten years from now, we just won't do business with people unless we're convinced they're paying their people a living wage' (Wise, 2021). He suggested that other firms would be shamed into following the firm's lead (Evans, 2021a). The Unilever initiative followed on from many years' collaboration with Oxfam (Wilshaw, 2021), building on an earlier commitment to introduce a living wage to its own employees: an initiative which took several years. In some ways it is surprising that it took the firm Unilever so long to address its own operations; however, the complexity of this was flagged up in research by Banaji and Hensman in 1990 (in a study of Unilever and Philips) which showed that although many aspects of firms' strategy and operations were managed centrally, detailed labour arrangements might often be left to local operating companies.

The announcement was widely reported but with many articles largely repeating material and quotes from Unilever's own press release, describing the initiative as being likely to 'help millions of workers out of poverty' (for example, Greedy, 2021). An Oxfam representative was quoted as saying, 'Unilever's plan shows the kind of responsible action needed from the private sector that can have a great impact on tackling inequality, and help to build a world in which everyone has the power to thrive, not just survive' (Forrest, 2021, p. 47). Walker (2021) described the announcement as 'a masterclass… a perfectly executed piece of ESG brand-building'. Analyst Lucy Ambler of Global Data characterized the move as excellent positioning 'ahead of the competitive CSR curve' (Briggs, 2021). In an advertisement in National Geographic ('paid content for Unilever'), the living wage initiative is framed as 'an upward spiral to a better life'—and passing reference is made to a separate philanthropic exercise in which the firm has temporarily transferred cash sums to women cocoa plantation workers in Cote D'Ivoire (although it is not clear what this has exactly to do with the living wage commitment: Heggi, 2022).[29] A Cambridge University researcher (funded by Unilever) commented, 'With the right momentum, the move by Unilever will stimulate a wider commitment to shifting labour market conditions towards the goal of 'decent work' for all' (Barford, 2021). Several newspaper headlines, and some reports, inaccurately implied that the firm was committing to 'everyone within its supply chain earning a living wage by 2030' (Barrie, 2021), missing the important qualification that the promise applied to the first tier. There appears to have been very little critical coverage of the announcement, apart from a right-wing 'think tank' blog, arguing against the very idea of firms seeking to manage their supply chain ('It's simply not going to work'; Worstall, 2021).

7.4   DISCUSSION

There are several aspects of Unilever's promise that are worth considering in detail. The commitment is distant and imprecise, overly optimistic in its effects, and entails no extra money for suppliers.

7.4.1   Distant and Imprecise

A virtue of Unilever's promise is that it specifies a date. However, the date by which the promise is to be achieved (nine years on) is a far away in corporate terms; at the time of the announcement, the average tenure for the 13 directors on the board firm was under five years; since 1988, only seven directors (out of the 60) have served on the board for nine years or more.[30] Given Jope's departure, by the time 2030 arrives, few of the existing senior leadership are likely to be in place.

The language deployed in the promise is also vague. There is no discussion of any potential commercial advantage to Unilever, nor any precise explanation as to the means of calculation that will be applied. The objectives are presented as 'a more equitable and inclusive society', complemented by an idea of 'driving the economic growth'. In a BBC (2021) report, the then chief of human resources is quoted as saying that 'Suppliers not willing to sign up *may* lose their contracts with the firm' (emphasis added). The firm's initial statement declares that 'we want to' [secure the Living wage for suppliers' workers] rather than 'we will'. The statement also contains a slight tension between the idea that this is something that will apply to all of the firm's suppliers, but that it will be 'specifically focusing' on vulnerable workers in manufacturing and agriculture. There is no sense of how the policy would operate given that the firm is involved in a regular churn of businesses it acquires and sells ('portfolio rotation': Morrison, 2022): if it takes nine years to implement the policy with existing suppliers, then would the suppliers to a newly acquired brand be given a similar time to comply? Indeed, the number of suppliers to whom the promise applies is not at all clear: the number cited varies from 'more than 60,000' (BBC, 2021); '60,000' (Everett, 2021); '56,300' (Unilever's 2021 Supply Chain Report); 'to around 53,000' (Unilever's 2021 Annual Report). Whatever the number, it seems unlikely that so many might be all handled by detailed collaborative arrangements which take into account specific local conditions; even a giant firm like Unilever would have insufficient procurement and supply chain specialists to go beyond programmatic and bureaucratic engagement in nearly all cases; 'working with suppliers' might, in this case, be slightly misleading.

The approach, by focussing on the employees of direct suppliers only, misses the fact that Unilever's supply chains will contain many tiers, with the most egregious exploitation often occurring several steps down the line. Even for direct suppliers, many agricultural workers will not in fact be employees of the suppliers, but contracted staff provided, for example, by labour providers; these are unlikely to be come under the purview of the scheme. It seems plausible that organizations could easily side-step the strictures of Unilever's demands by shifting to contract labour, or otherwise introducing another (perhaps artificial) 'tier' into the chain.

Unilever's promise also tacitly implies that workers who are directly involved in supplying Unilever will be covered by the commitment, but it is not clear if this means just those doing work that feeds through to Unilever, or whether it means all direct employees of the first-tier firms. Either inter-pretation is problematic; if the first, it requires suppliers to be able to identify workers who happen to be engaged in Unilever-related work, and to treat them differently from other workers (who might be doing exactly the same type of work but for other customers). This would appear to be practically impossible in many situations. The alternative, in contrast, creates significant impracticalities if the supplier firm has a large customer base, and what counts as the supplier. For example, although Unilever does not provide a general list of suppliers, it does do so for its palm oil procurement: one firm on this list is the giant food company, Associated British Foods (ABF). However, that firm currently has over four hundred subsidiaries and over 127,000 employees, and does not have a current living wage policy (although it has announced an aspiration to do so). Would Unilever cease to purchase from ABF unless all its subsidiary operations (most of whom would have nothing to do with supplying Unilever) complied with the living wage?

7.4.2   Overly Optimistic

The language used also draws a misleadingly rosy picture of what a living wage entails: it is claimed that it will enable workers 'to participate fully in their communities and help them break the cycle of poverty'. Whilst it is true that in some countries the effect would be substantial (because the gap between existing wages and the living wage is large) it is not the case that the living wage delivers some kind of economic nirvana; people will still be poor. The living wage may deliver more than existing minimum wages, and the rise may be significant and welcome, but it does not deliver prosperity. In countries where the gap between the official minimum wage and the living wage is small, the net effect may be meagre. In the UK, for example, the UK National Living Wage (i.e., the official minimum wage set by the government for those 23 years and older) is £9.50 per hour compared to the 'real' living wage (as set by the Living Wage Foundation, using the figure for outside of London) of £9.90, just 4.2% higher. Once tax is taken into account, this premium is reduced: if one assumes a 37.5-hour working week, the difference reduces to 3.2%. However, in the UK this pay is low enough to, in many cases, accrue modest government in-work benefits (depending on a range of complex factors, including housing costs, number of dependents et cetera), which diminish as income rises. This could, for example, reduce the net difference between those on the legal minimum and the 'real Living' wage to, say, just over 1%.[31] Life on the 'living wage' is still challenging, and, crucially, offers no possibility of meaningful accumulation. Despite the language used about 'a provision for unexpected events' or 'a bit of a buffer', there is in fact almost no margin for life's misfortunes. This is not to say that the marginal effect of the living wage is too small to bother with; it may matter a lot. But it is still not enough to provide what most of Unilever's Western customers would perceive to be a normal standard of living, and certainly not enough to warrant cosy, corporate smugness which portrays the living wage as an ethical panacea.

7.4.3   No Money for Suppliers

Crucially, Unilever's commitment does not explain where the money that pays for increased wages comes from. A reasonable person reading the Unilever's statements—with their air of moral heroism—might be forgiven for assuming that the initiative involved Unilever paying more money to suppliers, and then seeking to ensure that the money gets to workers. This important question was raised in the review by Morrison (2021), but receives a slippery answer:

> Asked if it will be increasing the amount it pays suppliers to cover the increase and how the living wage pledge among its suppliers will be policed, Unilever responded: 'We will engage with our suppliers, peer companies, NGOs and others to understand what needs to change in order to deliver this critical commitment. We believe that addressing social inequality and paying a living wage is a fundamental responsibility of businesses'.

Even Barford (2021), writing with enthusiasm about the initiative, leaves as a hanging question: 'How will higher labour costs be met?' Evans (2021a) reports Jope saying that the living wage policy would be funded by 'efficiencies elsewhere' – which might reasonably be taken to mean efficiencies within Unilever. However, in a passing meeting with him in September 2021, I had the opportunity to press this point, and to his credit the answer was clear and unapologetic. The initiative did not involve Unilever paying suppliers a penny more. The extra wages were to be funded by efficiency gains within the supplier and their own supply chains. Although this is not spelt out in Unilever's published material, it is a position consistent with the wording; Unilever haven't lied, but perhaps have been happy for their approach to be open to misinterpretation. The situation appears to mirror what Edwards et al. (2019, p. 16) find in regard to living wage initiatives in textiles; despite declared good intentions, firms 'are not modifying core purchasing practices'.

This key element of the initiative raises interesting points that have been largely neglected in the discussion of corporate-imposed living wages. Firstly, the initiative does nothing to address the issue of unequal exchange in supply chains. No marginal wealth is transferred from the consumer end of the chain to the producer end. Secondly, the approach is then open to important but unpredictable consequences. In the extensive literature on state-imposed minimum wages, an important idea is that the costs of minimum wages force employers to become more productive. This is called the 'shock theory':

> If a worker has to be paid £5 an hour instead of £4 an hour, the rational employer will seek to ensure that the worker becomes more productive so that it is worth paying that much for his or her output. This might involve investing in new machinery or providing training (Davies 2009, p. 141).

This argument has some plausibility and has featured in defences of minimum wages since the earliest debates ('High wages, too, it is shown by practical experience, lead to a lessening of the cost of production'; Snowden, 1912, p. 145). But there may be an element of wishful thinking here, as other alternatives might be available to the employer. For example, the higher wages might be achieved by: reducing non-wage benefits or the degradation of working conditions; the use of contracted/precarious (and thus non-regulated) labour; squeezing suppliers; and compromising on quality or safety. The initiative may also have complex effects in the situation where an affected firm—raising wages to meet Unilever's demands—then becomes uncompetitive in its ability to service other customers. Of course, it is also possible that, as with state-imposed minimum wages, positive 'spillover' effects mean that firms raise pay beyond the mandated level, or to groups of workers excluded from the legal requirement (Card and Kreuger, 1995; Teulings, 2003; Manning and Dickens, 2002).

The supplying firm also moves to a situation where decisions about its costs are externalised to an outside agency; this may be a problem if the firm cannot predict what changes will be made or when the changes will be made. For example, the official minimum wage in Tanzania stayed fixed for seven years before being raised in a single jump by over 23% (Mshomba, 2022). By adopting living wages, firms relinquish a degree of sovereignty in managing their own affairs, and in their ability to plan; this argument was central to the UK supermarket Sainsbury's rejection of activist pressure to adopt the living wage for its own employees (Jolly, 2022b).

The overall point to be made here is that Unilever's approach may or may not have desirable effects; understanding the impacts of state minimum wages has proven to be methodologically complex. It is very difficult to assess impacts without properly designed studies (Card and Kruger, 1995). The living wage concept seems to attract appealing, plausible arguments that often reflect hopes and prejudices more than careful deconstruction and empirical testing. Unfortunately, the ESG industry seems much happier with rating firms' (normally) self-reported virtue, rather than more tendentious and difficult-to-measure outcomes (Serafeim, 2021; Christensen et al., 2022).

7.5   CONCLUSIONS

In this final section, I suggest three propositions that emerge from the preceding discussion. They are intended to encourage and frame further research in this area.

7.5.1   Proposition One: Achieving Distributional Justice Cannot be Left to Large Corporations

The problematic nature of Unilever's supply chain living wage pronouncement does not mean that it is a bad thing, or that Unilever have acted in bad faith. But it does mean that we should be wary of hoping too much that firms that operate within the constraints of international capitalism might be able to bring reform from within. Simplistically: a fundamental problem with supply chain capitalism is that too much advantage has accrued to the rich consumers, and too little to the poor producers. Even mighty firms are too weak to buck the system, but it is important to understand the character of this weakness.

Unilever is certainly mighty. The argument that such firms are forced by consumer-market competition to constantly drive down prices, and thus have no option but to perpetually squeeze the supply chain does not quite hold up. In the inflationary crisis of the summer-autumn of 2022, Jope was found to be frequently reassuring investors that the firm was well-placed to raise prices in many of its markets, and that it could profitably forgo some volume in sales while retaining profitability; Unilever's vast scale means that it is one of the few food mega-companies that can engage in meaningful pricing negotiation with supermarkets. On one level, Unilever has the power to raise prices if it wanted to. Obviously, competition for consumers' money puts some limits on the extent to which firms can do this; if Magnum ice creams become too expensive, sales will naturally drop. But it is equally true to say that powerful companies have room for manoeuvre – and the point is that tiny increases in retail prices (if they could be transmitted to the base of supply chain) could have enormous effect. For example, the workers harvesting cocoa might receive less than a single percent of the cost of a chocolate bar.[32]

The issue, therefore, is not that consumers cannot afford to pay for decent work in supply chains; the issue is the mechanism of how money travels through the chain. Unilever's weakness is not that it is unable to set prices that could see that suppliers' workers are fairly paid—it is that it cannot break free from the patterns of commercial practice that define modern trade. This relates to the necessary realities of how procurement processes work between commercially independent entities. Without some kind of vertical integration, firms have, in reality, no option but to engage in commercial negotiation with suppliers – and it is this dynamic (not competition at the level of the end consumer) that results in unequal exchange and the inexorable processes that extract wealth from the poor to the rich. Special exceptions are always possible, as shown by the handful of initiatives regarding supply chain living wages mentioned above; but these are not scalable to the general case or business-as-usual. As long as firms such as Unilever are locked into the fundamental modus operandi of conventional procurement we should be sceptical of the prospects of corporations being effective instruments of distributive justice in supply chains. Buyers are not going to negotiate the best price, and then hand over extra money. In some cases, they perhaps can mandate specific wage levels, but they cannot avoid the risk of unintended consequences. This gloomy conclusion does not detract from the noble intentions of enlightened capitalism, but it does set a boundary on what is likely to be achieved. For distributive justice, we will have to look elsewhere.

7.5.2 Proposition Two: the Role of the State Must be to Redistribute Power

In the academic discussion of global supply chains, the state is often relegated to a minor or invisible actor. Indeed, one of the problems with the private regulation of supply chains is that it realigns the discourse to fit an often-unarticulated neoliberal orthodoxy: Dugger (1976, p. 314) argued that one function of the neo-classical model of the firm was to 'it defends the corporate system of economic power'. Importantly, he adds (p. 321) 'whether or not by conscious design'. Bowles (1974) discusses how professional economists can be 'servants of power' by rationalising the 'market' and problematising the 'state'. Unilever's pledge aligns with a tide of neoliberal orthodoxy in which the economic interest of society is dependent on the munificence of the powerful firm (Brown, 2003; Woodly, 2015). Much work in supply chain ethics reflects this paradigm: the roles of the state, the workers and global institutions are downplayed, and the agency of the corporation is uniquely valorised. But corporate power emerges in a context shaped by states, even in the Post-Westphalian era.

The fundamental problem in commercial exchange is power, which involves questions of inter-dependence, switching costs, investments and prevailing economic conditions—issues that are well-explored in the literatures or industrial economics and supply chain management. Despite some important differences, some of the same broad principles apply to the employment relationship; the outcome of exchange depends on the balance of power, and—because it depends on both buyers' and sellers' locus of alternative actions—is not just a function of the dyadic relationship. An important idea here is to look for what J.K. Galbraith labelled 'counter-vailing power' (Galbraith, 1952; Kesting, 2005). This means understanding the institutional arrangements that society imposes between trading partners, and between employees and employers, and the social context in which these mechanisms work.

In the supply chain context, weaker firms need protection: this means a potential role for the state in monitoring the commercial behaviour of large firms—something that already happens to an extent, but in a way that is widely regarded as feeble. For example, the UK government operates a small unit, the Groceries Code Adjudicator,[33] which seeks to monitor and restrain super-markets' abuse of their suppliers—many other countries have similar oper-ations. Other regulatory mechanisms include (also weak) devices to outlaw late payment (a practice for which Unilever has been criticised, and whose practices recently resulted in its removal as a member from a UK's Prompt Payment Code scheme; Hurley, 2022). Sharpening, extending and supporting these types of regulation—which up until now have most often relied on vol-untaristic participation by the regulated firms—could be an important step in rebalancing the power in supply chains. This would, however, require serious political intent and commensurate funding.

In the employment relation, the crucial issue is the existence of free asso-ciation, collective bargaining arrangements, and powerful and effective trades unions, underpinned by sound and enforced employment law. In the West, until recently, the long-term trend has been in both the radical decline of trade union power and the erosion of employment rights, and the under-funding to the point of evaporation of regulatory processes such as inspection. These prosaic and unglamorous measures are essential in providing the counter-vailing power. But strong unions and employment protection are only part of the answer.

LeBaron (2021) outlines three further relevant issues. Labour exploitation in supply chains reflects common patterns in which the overall situation of the exploited (which might, for example, be related to gender or migrant status) interacts with the demands of powerful supply chain customers. Following Crane (2013), LeBaron dismisses the idea that egregious labour conditions can be explained away by pointing to a limited number of bad actors. She highlights the 'porous' nature of extreme exploitation; workers suffer multi-faceted and interacting sets of disadvantages, with the unifying and enabling condition being poverty. Finally, she links these points to the ineffectiveness of buyer-driven governance efforts. Such schemes are too vulnerable to loop-holes and game playing, and do not address the fundamental issue: there is not enough money in the communities at the end of the chain. Hence, improving the general social well-being of the poorest, by means of social care, education, health provision and so on, is all part of the empowerment needed to redress imbalances of supply chain power. Workers can negotiate when they have options, but those experiencing general social deprivation have few. In other words, workers in the Unilever supply chain need more than an employer who will (somehow) give them just enough to get by; they need thriving communities, and negotiating power. Achieving supply chain justice relies on general social progress. Supply chain ethics does not dispense with the need for development economics and progressive politics: an overly hopeful focus on supply chain ethics may function as a kind of displacement activity for those seeking to work for social justice.

If we return to the early arguments made in the UK to support the introduction of the minimum wage, we see that they were deemed necessary in specific conditions: 'the unhealthy patches of the body politic', where 'healthy bargaining' was absent. Minimum wages—like Unilever's living wage promise—is a similar response to a symptom rather than the underlying disease.

7.5.3 Proposition Three: Even Progressive Firms Must be Subject to Critical Scrutiny

There is an argument that picking at claims made by firms like Unilever is foolish; even its harshest critics are likely to acknowledge that, in comparison to competitors, the firm has done many admirable things. However, we have ample evidence that big firms have a habit of conveniently forgetting promises, or using obfuscatory tactics to weasel out of commitments. For example, the Clean Clothes Campaign (2019) has accused the apparel firm H&M of making and then quietly deleting a supply chain Living Wage promise not dissimilar to Unilever's, and of making 'empty promises and bogus claims'.[34] In the environmental domain, Schacht (2022) reports on an investigation showing that that two-thirds of European firms' pledges on plastic packaging fail or are dropped. She gives the example of Danone's 2008 promise that within a year 50% of the firm's water bottles would be made from recycled plastic; by 2009 this had shifted to a 20 to 30% target for 2011, which it reached in 2020; the 50% target is now set for 2025. 'When companies fail to meet their pledges, they usually don't mention this openly. Instead, they silently drop the goal or shift its scope or target year' (Schacht, 2022). A European Commission investigation of green claims estimated a figure of 42% of firms' green claims were false or deceptive, and constituted unfair commercial practice.[35] I have argued elsewhere that to address these issues we need to radically rethink notions of corporate accountability and transparency, and to take seriously the means by which civil society can engage with and challenge corporate claims (Hsin et al., 2021; New, 2022). The analysis here suggests that Unilever's commitment is unlikely to represent a significant step in regard to supply chain exploitation. The propositions provide a modest framework for further research.

ACKNOWLEDGEMENT

The author would like to thank the following for their helpful comments on a draft of this chapter: Laurence Cranmer, Richard Cuthbertson, Alexander Trautrims, Lisa Hsin, and Athol Williams.

NOTES

1. https://twitter.com/Unilever/status/1352168701106253824
2. https://ourworldindata.org/human-development-index#standard-of-living
3. https://www.oecd.org/trade/topics/global-value-chains-and-trade/
4. https://www.worldbank.org/en/publication/wdr2020
5. https://www.ilo.org/global/research/global-reports/weso/2015-changing-nature-of-jobs/WCMS_368626/lang--en/index.htm
6. https://www.fdf.org.uk/fdf/resources/publications/reports/a-recipe-for-growth-prosperity-and-sustainability/
7. Firms which have made similar (but generally vaguer) commitments include Associated British Foods (https://www.abf.co.uk/content/dam/abf/corporate/Documents/Responsibility/2021-downloads/abf%20responsibility%20update%202021.pdf.downloadasset.pdf). Unilever's competitors Nestle have a living wage policy for their own employees, but only go as far as 'work to improve the livelihoods of farming families' in their supply chain (https://www.nestle.com/sustainability/human-rights/living-income).
8. https://www.unilever.com/brands/all-brands/. Mondelez have made a commitment that to 'work with our suppliers with the goal of having all our strategic suppliers engagement on a living wage roadmap by 2030' (Myers 2022). Neither Cargill nor Proctor and Gamble have made similar commitments.
9. https://www.unilever.com/news/press-and-media/press-releases/2020/unilever-sets-out-new-actions-to-fight-climate-change-and-protect-and-regenerate-nature-to-preserve-resources-for-future-generations/
10. https://packagingeurope.com/unilever-issues-update-on-packaging-goals/5300.article
11. https://www.business-humanrights.org/en/latest-news/unilever-still-selling-ice-cream-in-russia-despite-pledge-to-supply-essential-foods-only/
12. https://shareaction.org/news/unilever-shareholder-campaign-secures-industry-leading-transparency-on-nutrition
13. https://www.unilever.com/planet-and-society/equity-diversity-and-inclusion/transforming-our-brands-transforming-our-advertising/
14. Terry Smith, CEO Fundsmith, Letter to Shareholders, January 2022. 'Unilever seems to be labouring under the weight of a management which is obsessed with publicly displaying sustainability credentials at the expense of focusing on the fundamentals of the business. The most obvious manifestation of this is the public spat it has become embroiled in over the refusal to supply Ben & Jerry's ice cream in the West Bank. However, we think there are far more ludicrous examples which illustrate the problem. A company which feels it has to define the purpose of Hellmann's mayonnaise has in our view clearly lost the plot. The Hellmann's brand has existed since 1913 so we would guess that by now consumers have figured out its purpose (spoiler alert — salads and sandwiches).

Although Unilever had by far the worst performance of our consumer staples stocks during the pandemic we continue to hold the shares because we think that its strong brands and distribution will triumph in the end.' https://www .fundsmith.co.uk/media/3wcngjie/2021-fef-annual-letter-to-shareholders-web .pdf.

15. https://www.un.org/en/about-us/universal-declaration-of-human-rights
16. https://www.livingwage.org.uk/history
17. https://www.idhsustainabletrade.com/
18. https://www.globallivingwage.org/about/
19. https://actonlivingwages.com/
20. https://asia.floorwage.org/
21. https://cleanclothes.org/livingwage-old/calculating-a-living-wage
22. https://www .idhsustainabletrade .com/ publication/ eostas -sells -the -first -living -wage-mangoes/
23. https://www.tescoplc.com/blog/tesco-commits-to-paying-the-living-wage-gap -to-banana-producers/
24. https://www.baesystems.com/en-uk/article/living-wage
25. https://www .unilever .com/ planet -and -society/ raise -living -standards/ a -living -wage/
    Unilever Framework for Fair Compensation (June 2022). https://www.unilever .com/ files/ origin/ c95e3f7dfc 6a2c989121 33ea1e6058 1965fde340 .pdf/ Unilever %20Framework%20for%20Fair%20Compensation%202022.pdf
26. https:// www .unilever .com/ files/ 8f9a3825 -2101 -411f -9a31 -7e6f176393a4/ compass-strategy.pdf
27. https:// twinings .pinpointhq .com/ en/ jobs/ 60507; https:// assets .unilever .com/ files/92ui5egz/ production/6fd19e491d 1b12a1cf6d 0e26b79703 f31093ed6f.pdf/ responsible-sourcing-policy-interactive-final.pdf
28. https://www.unilever.com/news/press-and-media/press-releases/2021/unilever -commits-to-help-build-a-more-inclusive-society/
29. https:// 100weeks .org/ news/ magnum -and -100weeks -join -forces -again -in -awa -by-magnum-campaign
30. Source: FAME database (https://fame-r1.bvdinfo.com/).
31. Because of the many variables that come into play, it is quite difficult to derive a meaningful 'typical' number. Here I have taken the case of a single adult without disabilities or dependents in rented accommodation in a non-London high accommodation cost area (Oxfordshire), using the online calculators https:// www.moneysavingexpert.com/tax-calculator/ to calculate the impact of taxation, and https://www.entitledto.co.uk/ to calculate the effect of state benefits. The precise number can vary considerably depending on the assumptions made, but the general point holds.
32. Author's calculations based on available data; this type of calculation is often presented in terms of the share of the retail price that gets to the 'farmer' not the worker: see Nieburg (2014); Taylor (2020).
33. https://www.gov.uk/government/organisations/groceries-code-adjudicator
34. TurnaroundH&M (2018) sets out the way in which H&M's original 2013 com- mitment was reshaped.
35. https://ec.europa.eu/commission/presscorner/detail/en/ip_21_269

REFERENCES

Amin, S. (1976). *Unequal Development: An Essay on the Social Formations of Peripheral Capitalism.* Monthly Review Press.

Badenoch, K. (2022). Why I should become Prime Minister. *The Spectator,* 12th July. https://www.spectator.co.uk/article/read-kemi-badenoch-s-bid-for-prime-minister

Banaji, J., & Hensman, R. (1990). *Beyond Multinationalism: Management Policy and Bargaining Relationships in International Companies.* Sage.

Barford, A. (2021). Unilever makes global commitment to living wage. News: Cambridge Institute for Sustainability Leadership. 29th January. https://www.cisl.cam.ac.uk/news/blog/unilever-makes-global-commitment-to-living-wages

Barrie, L. (2021). Unilever takes social inequality stance with living wage commitment. JustFood.com, 21st January. https://www.just-food.com/news/unilever-takes-social-inequality-stance-with-living-wage-commitment/

BBC News (2021). Marmite maker Unilever to insist suppliers pay 'living wage'. BBC News, 21 January. https://www.bbc.co.uk/news/business-55735108

Boucoyannis, D. (2013). The equalizing hand: why Adam Smith thought the market should produce wealth without steep inequality. *Perspectives on Politics,* 11(4), 1051–1070.

Bowles, S. (1974). Economists as servants of power. *American Economic Review,* 64(2), 129–132.

Braithwaite, J. (2021). Ben & Jerry's gives Unilever an ice cream headache. *Financial Times,* 23 July. https://www.ft.com/content/1f89ac04-5a08-4297-9b6f-90d739211277

Blomberg, M. (2018). Stitched up? Fashion workers urge H&M to deliver living wage. *Reuters,* 18 December, https://www.reuters.com/article/us-cambodia-garment-h-m/stitched-up-fashion-workers-urge-hm-to-deliver-living-wage-idUSKBN1OH1CV

Brexendorf, T.O., & Keller, K.L. (2017). Leveraging the corporate brand. *European Journal of Marketing,* 51(9-10), 1530–1551.

Briggs, F. (2021). Unilever's living wage pledge is ahead of the competitive CSR curve, says GlobalData. *Retail Times,* 21 January. https://www.retailtimes.co.uk/unilevers-living-wage-pledge-is-ahead-of-the-competitive-csr-curve-says-globaldata/

Brock, J., & Geddie, J. (2022). Unilever's plastic playbook. *Reuters,* 22 June. https://www.reuters.com/investigates/special-report/global-plastic-unilever/

Brown, W. (2017). The toxic politicising of the national minimum wage. *Employee Relations,* 39(6), 785–789.

Brown, W. (2003). Neo-liberalism and the end of liberal democracy. *Theory and Event,* 7(1). https://muse.jhu.edu/article/48659

Butler, J. (2016). How the Tories use the language of social justice to sell us social injustice. Vice, 18 February. https://www.vice.com/en/article/9bjg9p/conservatives-use-the-language-of-social-justice-to-pursue-socially-unjust-policies

Byanyima, W. (2018). Supermarket supply chains are driving poverty: We can do better. World Economic Forum, 25 June. https://www.weforum.org/agenda/2018/06/supermarket-supply-chains-driving-poverty-inequality-winnie-byanyima-oxfam/

Campling, L., & Quentin, C. (2021). Global inequality chains: how global value chains and wealth chains (re)produce inequalities of wealth. In: Palpacuer, F. and Smith, A. (eds.), *Rethinking Value Chains: Tackling the Challenges of Global Capitalism,* 36–55, Policy Press.

Card, D., & Kruger, A.B. (1995). *Myth and Measurement: The New Economics of the Minimum Wage*. Princeton University Press.

CGD (2014). The surprising and sensible remarks of Unilever CEO Paul Polman. CGD Blog, 18 February. https:// www .cgdev .org/ blog/ surprising -and -sensible -remarks -unilever-ceo-paul-polman

Christensen, D.M., Serafeim, G., & Sikochi, A. (2022). Why is corporate virtue in the eye of the beholder? The case of ESG ratings. *The Accounting Review*, 97(1), 147–175.

Clean Clothes Campaign (2019). Not a single worker is making a living wage yet H&M claims to have done an amazing job. https://cleanclothes.org/news/2019/not-a-single -worker-is-making-a-living-wage-yet-hm-claims-to-have-done-an-amazing-job

CMF (2022). Under Wraps? What Europe's Supermarkets Aren't Telling Us About Plastic. Stichting Changing Markets, Utrecht. http:// changingmarkets .org/ wp -content/uploads/2022/05/Under-wraps_FULL-REPORT_FINAL.pdf

Coe, N., Hess, M., Yeung, W.C., Dicken, P., & Henderson, J. (2004). Globalizing regional development: a global production networks perspective. *Transactions of the Institute of British Geographers*, 29(4), 468–484.

Coneybeer, J., & Maguire, R. (2022). Evading responsibility: a structural critique of living wage initiatives and methodologies. *International Journal for Crime, Justice and Social Democracy*, 11(2), 15–29.

Corporate Knights (2021). Unilever to support 'living wage' and diverse suppliers. Corporate Knights, Spring, 15.

Crane, A. (2013). Modern slavery as a management practice: Exploring the conditions and capabilities for human exploitation. *Academy of Management Review*, 38(1), 49–69.

Craven-Matthews, E.L., Nordlund, A., & Fouzbi, Z. (2021). When Big Fish Eats Small Fish: The Acquisition of Ben & Jerry's by Unilever. LBMG Corporate Brand Management and Reputation-Masters Case Series. Lund, Sweden: Lund School of Economics and Management.

Dalmau, C.R. (2022). Different paths, common goal: How more companies are providing living wages. Sustainable Brands. https://sustainablebrands.com/read/supply -chain/ different -paths -common -goal -how -more -companies -are -providing -living -wages

Davies, A. (2009). *Perspectives on Labour Law*. Cambridge University Press.

Day, T., Mooldijk, S., Smit, S., Posada, E., Hans, F., Fearnehough, H., Kachi, A., Warnecke, C., Kuramochi, T., & Höhne, N. (2022). Corporate Climate Responsibility Monitor 2022. New Climate Institute, Cologne. https:// newclimate .org/ resources/ publications/corporate-climate-responsibility-monitor-2022

Deaton, A. (2013). *The Great Escape: Health, Wealth and the Origins of Inequality*. Princeton University Press.

Dobbins, T., & Prowse, P. (eds.) (2021). *The Living Wage: Advancing a Global Movement*. Routledge.

Doyle, J., Farrell, N., & Goodman, M.K. (2020). The cultural politics of climate branding: Project Sunlight, the biopolitics of climate care and the socialisation of the everyday sustainable consumption practices of citizens-consumers. *Climatic Change*, 163(1), 117–133.

Dugger, W.M. (1976). Ideological and scientific functions of the neoclassical theory of the firm. *Journal of Economic Issues*, 10(2), 314–323.

Edgecliffe-Johnson, A. (2022). The war on 'woke capitalism'. *Financial Times*, 27 April. https://www.ft.com/content/e4a818e5-4039-46d9-abe0-b703f33d0f9b

Edwards, R., Hunt, T., & LeBaron, G., (2019). Corporate Commitments to Living Wages in the Garment Industry. SPERI & University of Sheffield, Sheffield. http://mhssn.igc.org/Corporate%20commit%20-%20living%20wage%20-%20Sheffield%20-%20May%202019.pdf

Ehrenreich, B. (2001). *Nickel and Dimed: On (Not) Getting by in America*. Metropolitan.

Emmanuel, A. (1972). *Unequal Exchange: A Study of the Imperialism of Trade*. Monthly Review Press.

Ergon Associates (2015). Living Wages in Global Supply Chains: A New Agenda for Business. JETIs, London. https://www.ethicaltrade.org/sites/default/files/shared_resources/living-wages-in-global-supply-chains.pdf

Evans, J. (2021a). The shackles are off: Unilever goes for growth after UK move. *Financial Times*, 5 February. https://www.ft.com/content/66cc51f4-1ec3-4299-a7a7-ba152917947b

Evans, J. (2021b). Unilever's 'skin lightening' cream tests its purpose. *Financial Times*, 11 April. https://www.ft.com/content/7f8cb9a9-07f3-495e-8bac-4a071bfc64bd

Evans, J. (2022a). Unilever chief executive's pay jumps 42 per cent. *Financial Times*, 9 March. https://www.ft.com/content/abe9a428-5c94-44cc-82a3-c63885e3aad0

Evans, J. (2022b). Unilever raises prices by 8% and warns inflation will accelerate. *Financial Times*, 28 April. https://www.ft.com/content/a7a716cf-0f74-410b-a12d-fbcadb6ef4b9

Evans, J., & Agnew, H., Kuchler, H., Massoudi, A. (2022). Unilever bid fiasco ramps up pressure on managers to deliver plan B. *Financial Times*, 21 January. https://www.ft.com/content/7a1d6f47-90e0-4639-aed7-3817d4c18ed0

Evans, J., & Agnew, H. (2022). Big food's unhealthy products leave bitter taste for ESG investor. Financial Times, 4 June. https://www.ft.com/content/d04c3967-d0c8-4745-af17-62a1adc5a376

Evans, J., & Provan, S. (2022). Unilever to cut 1,500 jobs in management shake-up. Financial Times, 25 January. https://www.ft.com/content/0a08557a-7a2e-4ce3-8bfe-b4530c0a31cb

Evans, J., & Szalay, E. (2022). Activist investor Nelson Peltz to join board of Unilever. *Financial Times*, 31 May. https://www.ft.com/content/f7e72c63-9531-4d2b-9206-6e723dd1b3f0

Everett, C. (2021). Will Unilever kickstart a supply chain revolution? Raconteur, 24 March. https://www.raconteur.net/supply-chain/unilever-supply-chain/

Fieldhouse, D.K. (1978). *Unilever Overseas: The Anatomy of a Multinational 1895-1965*. Hoover Institution Press.

Fieldhouse, D.K. (1994). *Merchant Capital and Economic Decolonization: The United Africa Company 1929-1987*. Oxford University Press.

Filippino, M., Agnew, H., & Lewis, L. (2022). Discontent at Unilever. *Financial Times*, 24 January. https://www.ft.com/content/f5521873-501c-4b28-a2bf-3aba2f15fe3b

Financial Times (2019). Jobs are no longer a route out of poverty in the UK. *Financial Times*, 23 May. https://www.ft.com/content/d50bd4ec-7c87-11e9-81d2-f785092ab560

Fletcher, P. (2012). Private Member's Motion: Living Wage: A briefing note from the Mission & Public Affairs Council. GS1882B. Synod of the Church of England, London. https://www.churchofengland.org/sites/default/files/2018-01/gs%201882b%20-%20living%20wage%20pmm_Nov12.pdf

Forrest, A. (2021). Unilever commits to living wage for all the workers in its supply chains by 2030. *The Independent*, 22 January, p. 47.

Galbraith, J.K. (1952). *American Capitalism: The Concept of Countervailing Power.* Houghton Mifflin.

Gereffi, G., & Korzeniewicz, M. (eds.) (1994). *Commodity Chains and Global Capitalism.* Praeger.

Greedy, E. (2021). Unilever's living wage pledge could lift millions out of poverty. *HR Magazine,* January 25. https://www.hrmagazine.co.uk/content/news/unilever-s-living-wage-pledge-could-lift-millions-out-of-poverty

Heggi, J. (2022). Toward a living wage: What it is and why it matters. *National Geographic* (Paid content by Unilever). https:// www .nationalgeographic .com/ environment/article/paid-content-toward-a-living-wage

Henderson, J. (2022). How to spot strong company management. *Financial Times*, 17 June. https://www.ft.com/content/8b322f97-dfc1-4492-91b6-b77eb0bf3698

Hervey, G. (2020). Kenyan tea workers file UN complaint against Unilever over 2007 ethnic violence. *The Guardian*, 1 August. https:// www .theguardian .com/ global -development/2020/aug/01/kenyan-tea-workers-file-un-complaint-against-unilever -over-2007-ethnic-violence

Hickel, J., Dorninger, C., Wieland, H., & Suwandi, I. (2022). Imperialist appropriation in the world economy: drain from the global south through unequal exchange, 1990–2015. *Global Environmental Change*, 73, 102467.

Hodgson, C. (2021). Powerful investor group finds net zero pledges distant and hollow. *Financial Times*, 22 March. https://www.ft.com/content/12fd1c09-61fb-444e-a9cc -0b50fe0ea411

Hook, L. (2022). 'Net zero' plans by some of world's biggest companies accused of falling short. *Financial Times*, 6 February. https:// www .ft.com/ content/ db335e32 -74a6-48e5-94c8-7c6394100dc9

Hsin, L., New, S.J., Pietropaoli, I., & Smit, L. (2021). Accountability, Monitoring and the Effectiveness of Section 54 of the Modern Slavery Act: Evidence and Comparative Analysis. London: Modern Slavery Policy and Evidence Centre.

Humes, E. (2011). *Force of Nature: The Unlikely Story of Wal-Mart's Green Revolution.* Harper Collins.

Hurley, J. (2022). Unilever and Diageo 'too slow to pay small firms.' *The Times*, 3 March. https://www.thetimes.co.uk/article/unilever-and-diageo-too-slow-to-pay -small-firms-xsv0mzcwj

Jolly, J. (2022a). Sainsbury's CEO's pay triples to £3.8m as firm rejects living wage calls. *The Guardian*, 6 June. https://www.theguardian.com/business/2022/jun/06/ sainsburys-boss-pay-triples-to-38m-as-firm-rejects-living-wage-calls

Jolly, J. (2022b). Unilever chief Alan Jope to retire next year after five years at helm. *The Guardian*, 26 September. https://www.theguardian.com/business/2022/sep/26/ unilever-chief-alan-jope-retire-next-year-five-years-2023

Jones, G. (2005). *Renewing Unilever: Transformation and Tradition.* Oxford University Press.

Kesting, S. (2005). Countervailing, conditioned, and contingent – the power theory of John Kenneth Galbraith. *Journal of Post Keynesian Economics*, 28(1), 3–23.

Kumar, A. (2020). *Monopsony Capitalism.* Cambridge University Press.

LeBaron, G., (2021). The role of supply chains in the global business of forced labour. *Journal of Supply Chain Management*, 57(2), 29–42.

LeBaron, G., Edwards, R., Hunt, T., Sempéré, C., & Kyritsis, P. (2022). The ineffec- tiveness of CSR: Understanding garment company commitments to living wages in global supply chains. *New Political Economy,* 27(1), 99–115.

Lessenich, S. (2019). *Living Well at Others' Expense: The Hidden Costs of Western Prosperity*. Polity.

Lex (2022a). Unilever: New levers of growth fall short of a compelling pivot. *Financial Times*, 19 February. https://www.ft.com/content/859468f2-9473-4d42-aba6-24700914f5a8

Lex (2022b). Unilever/palm oil: Export ban latest blow as inflation looms large. *Financial Times*, 28 April. https://www.ft.com/content/0b3f39e5-3e09-4ca6-90d5-f5f13f3b3d07

Lex (2022c). Unilever: Ice cream split is the cherry on top of lacklustre management reshuffle. *Financial Times*, 25 January. https://www.ft.com/content/6f9a49ec-4dcf-4510-b8ad-9e714ddeaaa0

Mackey, J., & Sisodia, R. (2014). *Conscious Capitalism*. Harvard Business School Press.

Manning, A. and Dickens, R. (2002). *The Impact of the National Minimum Wage on the Wage Distribution, Poverty and the Gender Pay Gap*. London: Low Pay Commission.

Marlow, B. (2022). Unilever represents the decadent corporatism echoed by Putin's propaganda. *Daily Telegraph*, 10 March. https://www.telegraph.co.uk/business/2022/03/10/unilever-represents-decadent-corporatism-echoed-putins-propaganda/

Mayer, C. (2018). *Prosperity: Better Business Makes the Greater Good*. Oxford University Press.

Maynard, M. (2022). Is sustainability competing with price for priority? 10 charts explaining UK attitudes to the cost of living crisis? *The Grocer*, 26 August. https://www.thegrocer.co.uk/trend-reports/is-sustainability-competing-with-price-for-priority-10-charts-explaining-uk-attitudes-to-the-cost-of-living-crisis/670690.article

Miller, J., & Campbell, P. (2022). Unilever and Sanofi pile on pressure over 2035 EU petrol ban. *Financial Times*, 17 May. https://www.ft.com/content/32602ca3-4a97-46ca-bf78-2c2d0eb46979

Morrison, O. (2021). What to make of Unilever's commitment to living wage and diversity in its supply chain. *Food Navigator*, 21 January. https://www.foodnavigator.com/Article/2021/01/21/What-to-make-of-Unilever-s-commitment-to-living-wage-and-diversity-in-its-supply-chain#

Morrison, O. (2022). 'Rotation of our portfolio is part of upgrading into higher growth spaces': Unilever hints at food operation sell offs. *Food Navigator*, 17 January. https://www.foodnavigator.com/Article/2022/01/17/Rotation-of-our-portfolio-is-part-of-upgrading-into-higher-growth-spaces-Unilever-hints-at-food-operation-sell-offs

Mshomba, R. (2022). The minimum wage in real terms. *The Citizen*, 1 August. https://www.thecitizen.co.tz/tanzania/oped/the-minimum-wage-in-real-terms-3898850

Mundy, S., Temple-West, P., & Shimizuishi, T. (2022). What we learned from the IPCC report. *Financial Times*, 6 April. https://www.ft.com/content/b451075c-0ec1-4904-96c4-8ea0aa993a66

Murphy, H. (2020). Facebook wrestles with advertisers' demands as boycott escalates. *Financial Times*, 1 July. https://www.ft.com/content/2970cf91-dcf7-4424-bdc9-b6d92ad72d67

Myers, A. (2022). Mondelēz commits to living wage for cocoa farmers and invests in education programmes for children. *Confectionery News*, 22 July. https://www.confectionerynews.com/Article/2022/07/22/mondelez-international-commits-to-living-wage-for-cocoa-farmers-and-invests-in-education-programmes-for-children

Nathan, D., Bhattacharjee, S.S., Rahul, S., Kumar, P., Dahagani, I., Singh, S., & Swaminathan, P., (2022). *Reverse Subsidies in Global Monopsony Capitalism.* Cambridge University Press.

New, S.J. (2022). Modern slavery and supply chain transparency. In: Choi, T.Y., Li, J.J., Rogers, S., Schoenherr, T., Wagner, S.M. (eds.), *The Oxford Handbook of Supply Chain Management*, 101–130, Oxford University Press.

Nieburg, O. (2014). Paying the price of chocolate: Breaking cocoa farming's cycle of poverty. *Confectionery News*, 9 July. https://www.confectionerynews.com/Article/2014/07/10/Price-of-Chocolate-Breaking-poverty-cycle-in-cocoa-farming

Nillson, P., & Khan, M. (2020). Unilever's London-base move approved by shareholders. *Financial Times*, 12 October. https://www.ft.com/content/778716fd-ce5d-4bff-8706-43df5ae2687b

Phelps Brown, E.H., & Hopkins, S.V. (1955). Seven centuries of building wages. *Economica*, 22(87), 195–206.

Prapha, A. (2021). Global supply chains are broken; what's at stake at how to fix it. Oxfam. 21 October. https://politicsofpoverty.oxfamamerica.org/global-supply-chains-are-broken/

Prentis, D. (2016). How Osborne's fake 'Living Wage' could trap many in poverty. *Unison*, 27 January. https://www.unison.org.uk/news/2016/01/how-osbornes-fake-living-wage-could-trap-many-in-poverty/

Purves, L. (2022). Society pays the price for our cheap goods. *The Times*, 15 August, p. 25.

Raja, S. (2021). The Neoliberal 'Do-Good' Spirit: A Case Study of Unilever Digital Communication of Corporate Social Responsibility. Doctoral dissertation. Rutgers University.

Ramaswamy, V. (2021). *Woke, Inc.: Inside corporate America's social justice scam.* Hachette UK.

Reader, W.J. (1980). *Fifty Years of Unilever, 1930-1980.* Heinemann.

Schacht, K. (2022). European food companies break their plastics promises. 9 August. https://www.dw.com/en/european-food-companies-break-their-plastics-promises/a-62622509

Scharsig, M. (2016). Fast 10 Prozent der Studenten arbeiten noch unter Mindestlohn. 21 January. https://jobvalley.com/de-de/blog/fast-10-prozent-der-studenten-arbeiten-noch-unter-mindestlohn/

Schipani, A., Evans, J. & Wiggins, K. (2022). How Unilever's tea business became a test of private equity's conscience. *Financial Times*, 16 February. https://www.ft.com/content/0deba2c8-4a94-442e-8268-31586a5fb1ab

Selwyn, B. (2019). Poverty chains and global capitalism. *Competition & Change*, 23(1), 71–97.

Serafeim, G. (2021). ESG: hyperboles and reality. Harvard Business School Research Paper Series Working Paper, 22-031. https://www.hbs.edu/ris/Publication%20Files/22-031_b9b34057-062a-48a8-8950-61e0cf37559a.pdf

Snowden, P. (1912). *The Living Wage.* Hodder and Stoughton.

Stone, C., Trisi, D., Sherman, A., & Beltrán, J. (2020). A Guide to Statistics on Historical Trends in Income Inequality. *Policy Futures*, 13th January. https://www.cbpp.org/sites/default/files/atoms/files/11-28-11pov_0.pdf

Taylor, D. (2020). *The Invisible Women Behind our Chocolate.* Fairtrade Foundation.

Tennant, H.J. (1909). Speech at Second reading of Trades Board Bill. 28 April. Hansard. https://api.parliament.uk/historic-hansard/commons/1909/apr/28/trade-boards-bill

Teulings, C.N. (2003). The contribution of minimum wages to increasing wage inequality. *The Economic Journal*, 113(490), 801–833.

Timmins, B. (2022). Persil advert banned for misleading green claims. *BBC News*, 31 August. https://www.bbc.co.uk/news/business-62726666

Tsing, A. (2009). Supply chains and the human condition. *Rethinking Marxism*, 21(2), 148–176.

TurnaroundH&M (2018). Lost and Found: H&M's Living Wage Roadmap. https:// turnaroundhm .org/ static/ background -hm -roadmap -0f 39b2ebc333 0eead84a71 f1b5b8a8d4.pdf

Walker, C. (2021). The global Living Wage – Unilever's masterclass for ESG professionals. Responsible Investor. 5th February. https://www.responsible-investor.com/ the-global-living-wage-unilever-s-masterclass-for-esg-professionals/

Webb, S., & Webb, B. (1897). *Industrial Democracy*. Longman Greens and Co.

Wembridge, M. (2022). Ben & Jerry's sues owner Unilever over sale of Israel licence. *Financial Times*, 6 July. https:// www .ft .com/ content/ 2e9da02c -90f8 -490a -9122 -0de765da814e

Wilshaw, R. (2021). *How Oxfam Has Worked with Unilever to Enhance its Social Impact*. Oxfam.

Wilson, C. (1970). *The History of Unilever: A Study in Economic Growth and Social Change* (two volumes). Cassell.

Wilson, T. (2021). Shell wins backing of proxy advisors for move to UK. *Financial Times*, 26 November. https:// www .ft .com/ content/ 1e0378a7 -717f -4bbb -8822 -52d705d7ad87

Wise, H. (2021). Unilever demands all its suppliers pay workers the living wage by 2030 as boss says climate change and inequality are the world's two top issues. *This is Money*, 21 January. https://www.thisismoney .co .uk/ money/ markets/ article -9171307/Unilever-pledges-suppliers-pay-staff-living-wage.html

Woodly, D. (2015). *The Politics of Common Sense: How Social Movements Use Public Discourse to Change Politics and Win Acceptance*. Oxford University Press.

Worstall, T. (2021). Unilever's mistake about the supply chain. The Adam Smith Institute Blog, 22 January. https:// www .adamsmith .org/ blog/ unilevers -mistake -about-the-supply-chain

8. A just transition towards making precarious work rare, safe, and legal

Sandra L. Fisher, Annachiara Longoni, Davide Luzzini, Mark Pagell, Mike Wasserman and Frank Wiengarten

8.1 INTRODUCTION

Times of disruption offer an opportunity to think about what society expects from business in general and supply chains in particular. We observe that researchers and supply chain managers have, in a well-intentioned effort to maximize profit, inadvertently created conditions that have supported the spread of precarious work. Precarious work is characterized by wage inequality, unsafe workplaces, lack of worker voice, and a wide variety of costs and risks that are borne by workers and society (Allan et al., 2021). What drives precarious work? One piece of the puzzle is the rise of business school-trained managers who focus singularly on cost reductions, have been extracting rents at the expense of workers while not increasing revenues or profits (Acemoglu et al., 2022). Part of the problem is us.

We take a multi-level and cross-disciplinary conceptual approach to explore precarious work from the perspective of understanding the balance of power within the supply chain. This chapter examines precarious work at the societal and supply chain levels, highlighting the key issues of flexibility and cost management. We conclude by proposing some initial steps in a path for a just transition from the current state of workers all over the world facing low pay, hazardous working conditions, little voice in their own work environments, and a basic lack of dignity—to a less precarious workplace.

8.2 DEFINITION OF PRECARIOUS WORK

There have been recent calls to humanize the discipline of supply chain management (SCM) with a focus on working conditions or decent work (Soundarajan et al., 2021). Decent work is enshrined in the UN's Sustainable

Development Goals (Goal #8) and is defined by the ILO as involving 'opportunities for work that is productive and delivers a fair income, security in the workplace and social protection for families, better prospects for personal development and social integration, freedom for people to express their concerns, organize and participate in the decisions that affect their lives and equality of opportunity and treatment for all women and men' (ILO, 2022, para. 1). Decent work is a broad, multi-dimensional and aspirational construct.

Our focus is on one form of indecent work: precarious work. Common definitions include features of the work contract (duration of the contract, fixed term vs. ongoing, direct employment relationship vs. triangular) as well as working conditions (low wages, few benefits, few social protections, existence of collective bargaining or other representation; Allan et al., 2021; Kalleberg, 2009). Workers, not their employers, bear most, if not all, of the risk in jobs that lack certainty, stability, and security (Wiengarten et al., 2021; Kalleberg and Vallas, 2018). There are varying degrees of precarity with 'workers who have permanent employment, are well paid and have collective bargaining power being the least precarious and workers who have temporary employment, are poorly paid and have no collective bargaining power being the most precarious' (Wiengarten et al., 2021, p. 928). Precarity is not a binary characteristic but varies along a continuum. Workers who are day labourers, seasonal crop pickers, and food delivery riders or drivers are often considered among the most precarious. High-skilled professional gig work (e.g., freelance work involving software design, translation) is still precarious but can result in more decent work overall. Precarious work is not the sole barrier to decent work, but it is a significant barrier.

We focus our discussion of precarious work on the linkage between cost and flexibility across two levels of analysis: the supply chain and societal levels. The elements of precarious work are all directly linked to matching the supply of labour to uncertain demand, at the lowest possible cost. Precarious work is directly controlled by supply chain managers and links the supply chain and societal levels, while some other elements of decent work are mainly outside the control of supply chain managers and hence do not make these linkages. This is a critical point because it creates a supply chain specific lens through which we can more clearly explore the outcomes of precarious work.

8.3   OUTCOMES OF PRECARIOUS WORK

Supply chain-level discussions of precarious work tend to be inside-out; that is, the firm is the primary actor and profits remain a primary outcome of interest. For example, there is a long history of looking at flexible work as a means to meet scheduling variability in the operations management literature (e.g., Fredendall et al., 1996). Most of this research was done from a purely economic perspective and did not consider the very well-developed literature from outside supply chain management (e.g., in psychology, sociology, criminology, and labour/industrial relations) that makes it clear that these flexible jobs are frequently precarious and harm workers (Hashemi-Petroodi et al., 2021).

SCM research that focuses primarily on financial objectives generally concludes that adopting precarious work leads to improved supply chain outcomes (Hallgren and Olhager, 2009; Jack and Raturi, 2002). Much of this support came from modelling literature that suggested that capacity flexibility can be increased, and costs can be reduced by replacing permanent full-time workers with temporary or part-time workers which allows better alignment of demand and supply and acknowledges the difficulty in predicting demand accurately (Jack and Raturi, 2002). While temporary or part-time workers are not necessarily engaged in precarious work, often these are workers with lower hourly wages, fewer benefits, and little voice. From a supply chain perspective, precarious work provides a quick fix to potentially make supply chains more adaptive, aligned, and agile (Lee, 2004). However, newer research focused on supply chains built on the lean philosophy suggests that some of the recent disruptions that led to fluctuations in demand and supply, cannot be sufficiently mitigated through capacity flexibility. Cohen et al. (2022) suggest that disruptions that seem to be increasingly frequent require a resilient supply chain system that rests on complex capabilities rather than a pure lean approach.

Therefore, the conclusion from the early 21st century that adopting precarious work benefits both the firm and supply chain is now criticized as being overly simplistic, as it is strategically short-sighted and ignores workers (e.g., Simpson et al., 2021). Still, recent SCM research that does acknowledge problems of precarity (e.g., Wiengarten et al., 2021) continues to explore precarious work from the perspective of identifying when it makes sense for the supply chain to use such workers. For example, this research addresses questions of when it is in the supply chain's interest to use precarious workers, or how buying firms can ensure that suppliers provide appropriate working conditions while still meeting traditional supply chain goals related to cost, quality, and delivery. Inside-out research at the supply chain level that does acknowledge precarious work is thus focused on making these forms of work more effective for firms within the supply chain, and typically pays little attention when costs are shifted from the supply chain to society.

Discussions of precarious work at the societal level tend to be outside-in. That is, supply chain managers are still considered, but other actors such as regulators, NGOs, unions, and the workers themselves are prioritized, and working conditions are the primary outcome of interest. Outcomes of precarious work at the worker level have been studied extensively in the psychology, industrial relations, and sociology literature, with most of the outcomes such as lower job satisfaction, lower self-esteem, and higher levels of stress and burnout, viewed as negative for the individual (e.g., Allan et al., 2021). The psychology of working theory (Blustein et al., 2019; Duffy et al., 2016) focuses on decent work, suggesting that individuals who have decent work have higher need fulfilment through their work and experience better well-being. Positive outcomes of precarious work have been documented, primarily for higher-skill workers who enjoy the flexibility of work without the constraints of employment. Independent workers such as freelancers and gig workers experience greater levels of work autonomy, making their own choices about where, when, and for whom they work (Kuhn and Maleki, 2017). However, evidence suggests that 'the benefits of autonomy accrue to only the most skilled and fortunate among independent workers' (Petriglieri et al., 2018, p. 4). Many other ostensibly independent workers experience frustration, stress, and anxiety resulting from high levels of uncertainty (Schor et al., 2020).

Given these outcomes, outside-in discussions of precarious work tend to focus on how to improve working conditions in supply chains and are often centred on the perspective that decent work (Sustainable Development Goal 8) is a fundamental right, making precarious work inherently wrong. For instance, common good human resource management (HRM) acknowledges that firms have financial interests but defines the key concern of common good HRM as helping to solve grand challenges such as creating decent work (Aust et al., 2020). Equally, calls from within the supply chain discipline to humanize research on working conditions (e.g., Soundararajan et al., 2021) have treated decent work as the primary goal and frequently focused on actors such as the workers themselves (Reinecke and Donaghey, 2021) or unions (Kuruvill and Li, 2021). Outside-in research is then focused on eliminating precarious work.

8.4   MOVING TOWARDS SOLUTIONS: POWER, SUPPLY CHAINS, AND PEOPLE

Emotionally, the outside-in perspective resonates with us as we write this chapter. However, we realize that to better understand these issues requires explicating a pair of assumptions. The first is that within supply chains, there will always be the need for some workers to take on tasks that have uncertain hours and/or are of a short duration. That is, there will always be some work to be performed that could take on the form of precarious or indecent work.

Second, common good HRMs, or humanized supply chains (Aust, et al., 2020; Soundararajan et al., 2021), will require a combination of regulation and support at the societal level. Societies can and should put in place support so that workers in these jobs do not suffer the outcomes associated with jobs with precarious characteristics. This combination is sometimes referred to under the linguistically problematic banner of flexicurity (e.g., Wilthagan and Tros, 2004), referring to employment arrangements in which firms can implement the flexible solutions they need while also ensuring that workers have access to the security they need. Flexicurity attempts to bridge the gap between the inside-out and outside-in approaches and explores the space where society and supply chains intersect. But firms must worry about profitability and policy makers often do not.

Combined, these assumptions suggest that neither the goal of profit maximization (inside out) or the elimination of precarious work (outside in) can be universally pursued. Therefore, we use a cross-level perspective to rethink how the supply chain impacts jobs. The goal is that firms and customers can still reap the benefits of flexibility, without shifting most of the risks to precarious workers and most of the costs to society. We move closer to this goal by using a power perspective to explore precarious work taking both the supply chain and societal levels into account.

Power is fundamental to seminal SCM thinking such as the Kraljic matrix. Yet, precarious workers have little power, while consumer demands for low prices are a powerful force, and shareholder demands for profits are even more powerful. Pagell et al. (2010) applied the concepts of the Kraljic matrix and developed a modified sustainable purchasing portfolio model, concluding that 'when organizations pursue common prosperity as part of a larger effort to create a sustainable supply chain, they will make investments in supplier continuity that seem to contradict existing purchasing portfolio models' (p. 70). However, they incorporated mainly environmental factors in their analysis and explored the purchasing of physical goods rather than services or labour. We explicitly examine the people component. If buying firms are sometimes willing to help suppliers move out of a commodity trap, when and how might they be willing to help workers move out of a situation of precarious work? The result should be that precarious work still will exist but becomes, to borrow a phrase, rare, safe, and legal.

The governance of relationships is determined by power balances and imbalances between parties. For instance, worker-supervisor, buyer-supplier, firm-regulator represent relationships whose outcomes follow a given power distribution. Power is at the centre of supply chain relationships and thus has been the subject of much SCM research (e.g., Crook and Combs, 2007; Cox, 2001; Maloni and Benton, 2000; Reimann and Ketchen, 2017). Defined as one party's ability to enforce its will on another party (Emerson, 1962), power plays a key role in both the context of high dependence between buyers and suppliers (Terpend and Krause, 2015), and in collaborative relationships where jointly created value needs to be redistributed (Chicksand, 2015).

In the traditional 'command and control' view of supply chains, market-based power mechanisms prevail, leading managers to consider workers as resources that should be used efficiently. However, a recent call on working conditions in supply chains suggests to 'humanize' research and practice to achieve decent work (Soundararajan et al., 2021). Similarly, empirical evidence from social impact supply chains shows that focal organizations can re-orient key relationships toward alternative forms of power (Longoni et al., 2019). Authors usually distinguish forms of mediated power from nonmediated power (Benton and Maloni, 2005; Nyaga et al., 2013). The former entails the deliberate use of incentives (reward power) or punishments (coercive power). The latter, instead, depends on perceptions and cannot easily be controlled. Nonmediated power can be granted based on the identification with the counterpart (referent power), the recognition of its expertise (expert power), or the legitimation obtained through formal mechanisms (legitimate power).

A great deal of the SCM literature focuses on mediated power that results from the dependence of one party on another, in line with resource dependence (Pfeffer and Salancik, 1987) or social exchange theory (Blau, 1964). Despite mediated power having been recognized as potentially detrimental for trust, relationship commitment, and ultimately performance (Benton and Maloni, 2005; Terpend and Ashenbaum, 2012), few studies in the supply chain literature have explored alternative forms and uses of power. The supply chain literature is usually based on the premise that power serves to appropriate value. In contrast, we explore situations where the type of power and the way it is used can solve the challenges of precarious work. In this context, we expect that power will manifest in specific forms (i.e., nonmediated power) and in connection with other relational mechanisms, such as collaborative forms of governance.

8.5   A MULTI-LEVEL VIEW OF POWER

From the worker perspective, much research has examined how power and status predict the likelihood that individuals will be in the position of precarious work. Power and status operationalized through skill levels, immigration status, age, and gender are all associated with a higher likelihood of engaging in precarious work (Agarwala, 2019; Alberti et al., 2013; Monteith and Giesbert, 2017). These workers are often then dependent on the jobs they can find, in spite of them being low quality. When precarious workers have relatively low levels of skills they have few other alternatives for work, and thus become even more dependent on the employers offering precarious work. Such dependence further serves to reduce the power these workers might exercise to improve their working conditions. Workers who freely choose precarious work because of perceived advantages such as flexibility (i.e., skilled platform work) are likely to have higher power and status in the employment relationship. Unions in some countries have been able to make gains in reducing precarity (Carver and Doellgast, 2021; O'Brady, 2021), but institutional power may limit the ability of unions to exert their power on behalf of workers in precarious jobs.

Weakened unions in some regions of the world (e.g., United States, Brazil) have also resulted in lower power for unions and fewer worker protections. There are many restrictions around the world in the extent to which precarious workers are permitted to join unions, or if they are legally permitted to join, if they actually have the opportunity. Thus, the instrument of unionization is often unavailable for increasing power on behalf of precarious workers.

When considering power at the supply chain level, we turn our attention to inter-organizational relationships. In sectors like fashion or food, we often observe an imbalance between the excessive power of large global buyers in their relationship with small manufacturers and producers. Such an imbalance is usually exercised to subtract benefits from less powerful actors, thus becoming a determinant of precarious work at specific stages of the supply chain. Examples range from worker exploitation and violation of basic rights in the upstream garment manufacturing supply chain (Kelly, 2021; Greenpeace, 2022) to the inhumane pickers' conditions in Italy or Spain (Di Donato, 2021; De Pablo et al., 2020). To address these gaps, new regulations are proposed to hold focal companies accountable (Paton, 2022). However, there are different approaches to dealing with power imbalances within the supply chain when the level of analysis shifts to the country or societal level.

At the societal level, governments have the legitimate power to introduce regulations to reduce precarity or improve the quality of precarious work. However, trends in neoliberalism have resulted in a general reduction in worker protections and an associated rise in precarity around the world (Kalleberg and Hewison, 2013). As regulation has declined, precarious work has increased even when overall incomes are rising. Even when countries establish laws limiting precarity, many employers engage in 'institutionalized toying', or inventing avenues to get around the laws to make work more precarious and less decent (Benassi and Kornelakis, 2021). For example, firms may take advantage of legal loopholes or ambiguities to classify parcel delivery or call centre workers as self-employed or subcontracted, even when the work relationship includes employment-oriented features such as direct instructions on how to perform the work. This is a good starting point to explore the power dynamics between supply chains and society.

Power seems to be asymmetrically oriented against workers in many contexts. However, we find some interesting elements of the relationships across levels of economic activity and precarious work by exploring the power balance at the intersection of the supply chain and societal levels of analysis. Figure 8.1 outlines where the costs and benefits of precarious work are borne and when rent seeking elements of the supply chain have more power than those elements that prioritize human and social elements. In the top figure, workers in precarity shoulder the balance of costs. Society bears much of the remainder. Firms and their shareholders shoulder a small segment of the human- and society-oriented cost burden but benefit from the flexibility and lower costs. Customers gain the benefits of low-priced products available when and where they are desired at a low price. The lower half of Figure 8.1 shows the relationship when power is more balanced between rent seeking and socially aware elements of the supply chain. Costs are more fairly distributed, with workers shouldering less of a burden. Customers pay slightly higher prices and shareholders earn slightly lower returns. However, long-run externalities are not hidden and, it can be argued, are less expensive to manage in the long run through better prevention of individual and social problems related to precarity.

8.6   THREE EXAMPLE SOLUTIONS

We offer three examples of solutions to reduce the amount of precarious work, or at least to reduce the level of precarity within such jobs. The goal is to make the use of precarious work rare, safe, and legal. All three of these examples use relational mechanisms, such as collaborative forms of governance, to shift the power dynamics in such a way that costs and benefits are shared across levels of the system.

First, there is a clear need for both supply chain managers and researchers to connect physical goods supply chains with labour supply chains. This connection is rarely made in the SCM literature. Rare exceptions include some of the work on audits (Bird et al., 2019) and work that shows that codes of conduct create conflicting pressures at the intersection of physical and labour supply chains (LeBaron and Lister, 2015). But in general, even when research integrates the two supply chains, recommendations are mostly absent. Linking the two supply chains together allows more transparency and accurate decisions.

One important possible solution is to understand that sourcing decisions need to be seen as job design decisions. That is, when employers need temporary or flexible work, sourcing managers can determine the type of tasks that need to be completed, the skills and number of hours needed, and the way in which the worker interacts with the tasks, to most effectively meet those needs without turning flexible work into precarious work. The practical implication of this for supply chains is that when a sourcing manager decides about labour needs, they are in effect exercising position power to make job design decision for suppliers. Physical supply chain decisions have an impact on the human attributes of the supply chain as well. In other words, choices about raw materials, subassemblies, manufacturing methods, channel, and delivery mechanisms all create constraints about the working conditions for the labour supply chain. Failure to consider this often leads to precarious working conditions. We know that certain jobs are already designed to be self-contained and then moved outside the organization, outsourced to a lower cost provider

Current State: Power asymmetry in favor of rent seeking supply chain partners

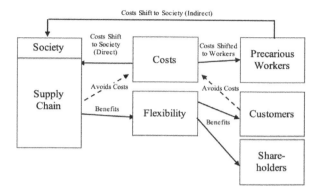

Desired State: Power asymmetry minimized through shared governance and other functions that seek to attain a less precarious world

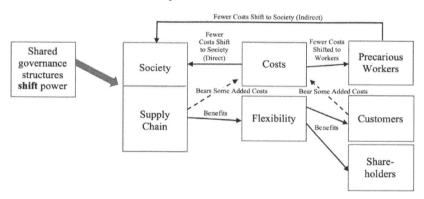

Figure 8.1   Power asymmetry, precarious work and the balance between rent-seeking supply chains and betterment-seeking societal elements, including workers

(Benassi and Kornelakis, 2021). Sourcing managers should consider how their requirements affect job design, and to what extent their requirements limit the ability of suppliers to make work less precarious. A first step in this process could be to use cost models to determine the wages or working condition a supplier could offer given the specifications and unit price; especially since in many cases the answer will indicate that it is impossible to meet the demands of the physical supply chain without creating labour precarity (e.g., Hasan et al., 2020).

Further, demand-side job characteristics should be balanced with more micro-level job design features to produce more meaningful, more decent work arrangements. From the industrial or organizational psychology literature, good job design includes thinking about five specific job characteristics: skill variety, task identity, task significance, autonomy, and job-based feedback (Hackman and Oldham, 1975; Ilgen and Hollenbeck, 1991; Oldham and Fried, 2016). Quite often, skill variety is reduced in work considered suitable for temporary or flexible work, but sourcing managers could consider how to make individual tasks more complete so there is identity, some feedback that comes directly from the work, and an opportunity for some autonomy within performance of the work.

Second, jobs that require flexibility can use a private or public-private solution like the construction trade union model in the United States to help balance the power between the supply chain and the worker. There is also a rich literature documenting the concept of worker cooperatives in diverse settings such as home health care (Berry and Bell, 2018) the Nigerian informal economy (Osiki, 2020), and online labour platforms, including a study by Reinecke and Donaghy (2021) discussing an emerging development in worker-driven supply chain governance. These organizations can help solve flexibility issues from the employer side with a much lower total cost (supply chain + worker + society) even though the supply chain bears a slightly higher wage rate. A cooperative model suggests that human resources are shared among employers as needed. Workers get a fair wage, a portable pension, health insurance (e.g., in the United States), training, skills upgrading, certifications, and other benefits that normally are not available to temporary or other precarious workers. A tool such as the German Arbeitszeitkonto (working-time account) could be implemented across employers within a supply chain, allowing workers to smooth their earnings, even when working hours are unbalanced across weeks or months. When workers have the benefits of less precarious work, costs to society are lower. These costs could be offset by policy-based incentives. This solution, already in place for some higher-skilled workers, can work in a variety of industries.

Third, another example of supply chain-level commitments to reducing precarity is emerging regarding compensation. This model is used by competitors who collaborate for the common good, essentially giving up some of their own individual power for the benefit of the entire supply chain, including individual workers. There are many examples of rivals working together in this manner to reduce harmful elements of raw materials, but not so many on the human side. In one example, the German Retailers Working Group on Living Income and Living Wages, representing retail chains such as ALDI, Lidl, and Kaufland, is working toward achieving a living income for farmers and workers in the food supply chain, developing and testing more sustainable practices. In doing so, these firms may give up some advantage that could be attained through sources of mediated power, but replace them with expert or legitimate power developed through the cooperative research effort.

8.7   CONCLUSIONS

We can only address precarious work effectively when we look at all relevant stakeholders and identify salient costs and benefits in both the short and long run (see for example Mitchell et al., 1997). By exploring the power relationships among stakeholders, we can conclude that society is a dormant stakeholder. Society has the ability but often chooses not to enact policy to reduce precarity. We recognize the existence of conflicting perspectives and stakeholder groups, with dynamics related to power that inhibit action to protect individual workers. That said, reducing precarity is beneficial first and foremost to the individual, and the benefits do not accrue across the supply chain. Meanwhile, firms almost always act in self-interest. While there are a few exemplars pointing toward a transition away from precarity, these are few and far between. The result of inaction by firms, supply chains, and societal institutions is that workers, and society more broadly, pay the price, especially in the long run. So, with more transparency, will social norms change to reduce the acceptability of precarious work? This is an open question, but our analysis suggests that it is of critical importance to create conversations that are not about either profits or people, but about making a just transition to a world where worker precarity is reduced. A zero-sum conversation where we eliminate either precarious work or corporate profits is not productive. We need to emphasize the middle ground, where stakeholders understand the costs and benefits of precarity, where we can separate the notion of flexibility from low costs, and where, through a combination of incentives, policy, social norms of ethical behaviour, and consumer action, we can get to a better place than where we are now.

Putting this question in more concrete terms leads us to six conclusions:

1. Temporary contracts are probably justified in limited situations.
2. A world without precarious jobs is probably not a reasonable expectation.
3. We can move toward a world where some precarious work is pragmatically acceptable when companies that benefit bear the costs, instead of workers themselves.
4. We can, in the short run at least, accept temporary work, as long as it is well-paid and safe.

5.   We can live in a world where power is more in balance and costs and benefits are more evenly shared, without great harm to any one group of stakeholders by supporting coordination within and across supply chains. We need to focus on how to prevent precarious jobs from bleeding into precarious lives.

6.   We can do this through a combination of creative programs that are driven by incentives, supply-chain wide initiatives, and government safety nets, perhaps with some public-private partnerships where feasible.

Addressing this important issue of precarious work, where the well-being of many is at risk every single day, is a critical need. We think it is possible to move quickly and make tangible progress toward making a just transition to a less precarious world.

REFERENCES

Acemoglu, D., He, A., & le Maire, D. (2022). Eclipse of Rent-Sharing: The Effects of Managers' Business Education on Wages and the Labor Share in the US and Denmark (No. w29874). National Bureau of Economic Research.

Alberti, G., Holgate, J., & Tapia, M. (2013). Organising migrants as workers or as migrant workers? Intersectionality, trade unions and precarious work. *The International Journal of Human Resource Management*, 24(22), 4132-4148.

Allan, B.A., Autin, K.L., & Wilkins-Yel, K.G. (2021). Precarious work in the 21st century: A psychological perspective. *Journal of Vocational Behavior*, 126, 103491.

Agarwala, R. (2019). Using legal empowerment for labour rights in India. *The Journal of Development Studies*, 55(3), 401-419.

Aust, I., Matthews, B., & Muller-Camen, M. (2020). Common Good HRM: A paradigm shift in Sustainable HRM? *Human Resource Management Review*, 30(3), 100705.

Benassi, C., & Kornelakis, A. (2021). How do employers choose between types of contingent work? Costs, control, and institutional toying. *ILR Review*, 74(3), 715-738.

Berry, D., & Bell, M.P. (2018). Worker cooperatives: alternative governance for caring and precarious work. *Equality, Diversity and Inclusion: An International Journal*, 37(4), 376-391.

Benton, W.C., & Maloni, M. (2005). The influence of power driven buyer/seller relationships on supply chain satisfaction. *Journal of Operations Management*, 23(1), 1-22.

Bird, Y., Short, J.L., & Toffel, M.W. (2019). Coupling labor codes of conduct and supplier labor practices: The role of internal structural conditions. *Organization Science*, 30(4), 847-867.

Blau, P.M. (1964). *Exchange and Power in Social Life*. John Wiley & Sons, Inc.

Blustein, D.L., Kenny, M.E., Di Fabio, A., & Guichard, J. (2019). Expanding the impact of the psychology of working: Engaging psychology in the struggle for decent work and human rights. *Journal of Career Assessment*, 27(1), 3-28.

Carver, L., & Doellgast, V. (2021). Dualism or solidarity? Conditions for union success in regulating precarious work. *European Journal of Industrial Relations*, 27(4), 367-385.

Chicksand, D. (2015). Partnerships: The role that power plays in shaping collaborative buyer–supplier exchanges. *Industrial Marketing Management*, 48, 121-139.

Cohen, M.A., Cui, S., Doetsch, S., Ernst, R., Huchzermeier, A., Kouvelis, P., ... & Tsay, A. (2022). Bespoke Supply Chain Resilience: The Gap between Theory and Practice. *Journal of Operations Management*, 86(5), 515-531.

Cox, A. (2001). Managing with power: strategies for improving value appropriation from supply relationships. *Journal of Supply Chain Management*, 37(2), 42.

Crook, T.R., & Combs, J.G. (2007). Sources and consequences of bargaining power in supply chains. *Journal of Operations Management*, 25(2), 546-555.

De Pablo, O., Zurita, J., Kelly, A., & Carlile, C. (2020). 'We pick your food': migrant workers speak out from Spain's 'Plastic Sea'. *The Guardian*, September 20. https://www.theguardian.com/global-development/2020/sep/20/we-pick-your-food-migrant-workers-speak-out-from-spains-plastic-sea

Di Donato, V. (2021). How the pandemic helped gangmasters exploit the invisible agricultural workers of Italy. *Forbes*, April 2. https://www.forbes.com/sites/valentinadidonato/2021/04/02/how-the-pandemic-helped-gangmasters-exploit-the-invisible-agricultural-workers-of-italy/?sh=3fb3da1f169a

Duffy, R.D., Blustein, D.L., Diemer, M.A., & Autin, K.L. (2016). The psychology of working theory. *Journal of Counseling Psychology*, 63(2), 127.

Emerson, R.M. (1962). Power-dependence relations. *American Sociological Review*, 27(1), 31-41.

Fredendall, L.D., Melnyk, S.A., & Ragatz, G. (1996). Information and scheduling in a dual resource constrained job shop. *International Journal of Production Research*, 34(10), 2783-2802.

Greenpeace (2022). Cambodia workers pay the price of Fast Fashion's supply chain waste problem. https://www.greenpeace.org/international/story/55134/cambodia-workers-pay-the-price-of-fast-fashions-supply-chain-waste-problem/

Hackman, J.R., & Oldham, G.R. (1975). Development of the job diagnostic survey. *Journal of Applied Psychology*, 60(2), 159.

Hallgren, M., & Olhager, J. (2009). Flexibility configurations: Empirical analysis of volume and product mix flexibility. *Omega*, 37(4), 746-756.

Hasan, R., Moore, M., & Handfield, R. (2020). Addressing social issues in commodity markets: Using cost modeling as an enabler of public policy in the Bangladeshi apparel industry. *Journal of Supply Chain Management*, 56(4), 25-44.

Hashemi-Petroodi, S.E., Dolgui, A., Kovalev, S., Kovalyov, M.Y., & Thevenin, S. (2021). Workforce reconfiguration strategies in manufacturing systems: a state of the art. *International Journal of Production Research*, 59(22), 6721-6744.

Ilgen, D.R., & Hollenbeck, J.R. (1991). Job design and roles. *Handbook of Industrial and Organizational Psychology*, 2, 165-207.

ILO (2022). Decent Work. https://www.ilo.org/global/topics/decent-work/l—g--en/index.htm

Jack, E.P., & Raturi, A. (2002). Sources of volume flexibility and their impact on performance. *Journal of Operations Management*, 20(5), 519-548.

Kalleberg, A.L. (2009). Precarious work, insecure workers: Employment relations in transition. *American Sociological Review*, 74(1), 1-22.

Kalleberg, A.L., & Hewison, K. (2013). Precarious work and the challenge for Asia. *American Behavioral Scientist*, 57(3), 271-288.

Kalleberg, A.L., & Vallas, S.P. (2018). Probing precarious work: Theory, research, and politics. *Research in the Sociology of Work*, 31(1), 1-30.

Kelly, A. (2021). Top fashion brands face legal challenge over garment workers' rights in Asia. *The Guardian*, July 9. https://www.theguardian.com/global-development/2021/jul/09/top-fashion-brands-face-legal-challenge-over-garment-workers-rights-in-asia

Kuhn, K.M., & Maleki, A. (2017). Micro-entrepreneurs, dependent contractors, and instaserfs: Understanding online labor platform workforces. *Academy of Management Perspectives*, 31(3), 183-200.

Kuruvilla, S., & Li, C. (2021). Freedom of association and collective bargaining in global supply chains: a research agenda. *Journal of Supply Chain Management*, 57(2), 43-57.

LeBaron, G., & Lister, J. (2015). Benchmarking global supply chains: the power of the 'ethical audit' regime. *Review of International Studies*, 41(5), 905-924.

Lee, H.L. (2004). The triple-A supply chain. *Harvard Business Review*, 82(10), 102-113.

Longoni, A., Luzzini, D., Pullman, M., & Habiague, M. (2019). Business for society is society's business: Tension management in a migrant integration supply chain. *Journal of Supply Chain Management*, 55(4), 3-33.

Maloni, M., & Benton, W.C. (2000). Power influences in the supply chain. *Journal of Business Logistics*, 21(1), 49-74.

Mitchell, R.K., Agle, B.R., & Wood, D.J. (1997). Toward a theory of stakeholder identification and salience: Defining the principle of who and what really counts. *Academy of Management Review*, 22(4), 853-886.

Monteith, W., & Giesbert, L. (2017). 'When the stomach is full we look for respect': perceptions of 'good work' in the urban informal sectors of three developing countries. *Work, Employment and Society*, 31(5), 816-833.

Nyaga, G.N., Lynch, D.F., Marshall, D., & Ambrose, E. (2013). Power asymmetry, adaptation and collaboration in dyadic relationships involving a powerful partner. *Journal of Supply Chain Management*, 49(3), 42-65.

O'Brady, S. (2021). Fighting precarious work with institutional power: Union inclusion and its limits across spheres of action. *British Journal of Industrial Relations*, 59(4), 1084-1107.

Oldham, G.R., & Fried, Y. (2016). Job design research and theory: Past, present and future. *Organizational Behavior and Human Decision Processes*, 136, 20-35.

Osiki, A. (2020). 'Esusu cooperative' as a means of extending social protection to the Nigerian informal economy. *Contemporary Social Science*, 15(4), 461-475.

Pagell, M., Wu, Z., & Wasserman, M.E. (2010). Thinking differently about purchasing portfolios: an assessment of sustainable sourcing. *Journal of Supply Chain Management*, 46(1), 57-73.

Paton, E. (2022). New laws trying to take the anxiety out of shopping. *New York Times*, September 30. https://www.nytimes.com/2022/09/30/fashion/fashion-laws-regulations.html

Petriglieri, G., Petriglieri, J.L., & Wood, J.D. (2018). Fast tracks and inner journeys: Crafting portable selves for contemporary careers. *Administrative Science Quarterly*, 63(3), 479-525.

Pfeffer, J., & Salancik, G.R. (1987). A resource dependence perspective. In: Mizruchi, M. S., & Schwartz, M. (eds), *Intercorporate Relations. The Structural Analysis of Business*, Cambridge University Press, 25-55.

Reimann, F., & Ketchen Jr, D.J. (2017). Power in supply chain management. *Journal of Supply Chain Management*, 53(2), 3-9.

Reinecke, J., & Donaghey, J. (2021). Towards worker-driven supply chain governance: developing decent work through democratic worker participation. *Journal of Supply Chain Management*, 57(2), 14-28.

Schor, J.B., Attwood-Charles, W., Cansoy, M., Ladegaard, I., & Wengronowitz, R. (2020). Dependence and precarity in the platform economy. *Theory and Society*, 49(5), 833-861.

Simpson, D., Segrave, M., Quarshie, A., Kach, A., Handfield, R., Panas, G., & Moore, H. (2021). The role of psychological distance in organizational responses to modern slavery risk in supply chains. *Journal of Operations Management*, 67(8), 989-1016.

Soundararajan, V., Wilhelm, M.M., & Crane, A. (2021). Humanizing research on working conditions in Supply chains: Building a path to decent work. *Journal of Supply Chain Management*, 57(2), 3-13.

Terpend, R., & Ashenbaum, B. (2012). The intersection of power, trust and supplier network size: Implications for supplier performance. *Journal of Supply Chain Management*, 48(3), 52-77.

Terpend, R., & Krause, D.R. (2015). Competition or cooperation? Promoting supplier performance with incentives under varying conditions of dependence. *Journal of Supply Chain Management*, 51(4), 29-53.

Wiengarten, F., Pagell, M., Durach, C.F., & Humphreys, P. (2021). Exploring the performance implications of precarious work. *Journal of Operations Management*, 67(8), 926-963.

Wilthagen, T., & Tros, F. (2004). The concept of 'flexicurity': a new approach to regulating employment and labour markets. *Transfer: European Review of Labour and Research*, 10(2), 166-186.

PART III

Ways out of the crisis

9. Humanitarian supply chains: challenging the system

Gyöngyi Kovács and Graham Heaslip

9.1 INTRODUCTION

Humanitarian supply chains are not just another application area of supply chain management (SCM), but the context fundamentally alters some of the fundamental assumptions of SCM. It starts with challenging the notion of customers, extends to what is being delivered and considered a material flow, and the context even challenges the way we look at and use technology in the supply chain. This chapter analyses how humanitarian supply chains alter and challenge supply chains as a 'system in crisis'.

Saving lives and improving livelihoods is at the core of humanitarian supply chains, as to say that the main focus is on the social sustainability of SCM. Already in this, humanitarian supply chains challenge the mainstream view on SCM. Even sustainable SCM has for a long time typically focused on the natural environment mostly, albeit this is slowly changing, with topics ranging from modern slavery to the bottom of the pyramid, or supply chains in emerging economies (Seuring et al., 2022). Interestingly, humanitarian supply chains can be criticised for the opposite; their strong focus on saving lives can be at odds with ecological considerations. This is somewhat surprising when considering the relationship between climate change and natural disasters; and yet, the greening of humanitarian supply chains is a relatively new area of interest (Altay et al., 2021).

More parallels can be drawn between humanitarian and public health supply chains (Kovács and Falagara Sigala, 2021). This includes the discussion on whether beneficiaries or patients are to be seen as customers in light of a decoupling of financial from material flows in both. After all, purchasing power comes with the possibility to vote with one's feet (or money), be able to make one's own prioritisation, and move to another provider or product or other service offerings if needed. Such purchasing power is limited in the case of receiving aid. That said, systemic change is around the corner, with cash and vouchers replacing items that are being delivered as humanitarian aid (Maghsoudi et al., 2023). Cash-based initiatives fundamentally alter humanitarian supply chains, which is why cash as an innovation is regarded a paradigm shift (Altay et al., 2023).

There are plenty of other innovations in humanitarian supply chains, across all dimensions from new products to new services, new processes, and new paradigms (Altay et al., 2023). As innovation research tends to do, all of them claim to revolutionise the field. As in SCM overall, everything from blockchains to additive manufacturing to industry 4.0 have found their way to humanitarian supply chains as well. And while many of them are applicable in, for example, a flood, there are other situational contexts of humanitarian supply chains in which their applicability can be more limited. After all, tracking and tracing material flows in a warzone can also make them more susceptible to attacks; and how should beneficiaries distinguish between a drone that is used by the military from one that delivers aid (van Wynsberghe and Comes, 2020)? At the same time, the use of social media data can be misleading without a proper vulnerability capacity assessment that verifies the claims of people of needing aid; and the newest types of trucks may not be operable in remote locations with a destabilised transport infrastructure. Technology is only a bliss if circumstances allow it.

This chapter, thus, investigates three ways in which humanitarian supply chains challenge premises from SCM: greening, cash, and technological change. Greening efforts widen the perspective on the system and investigate the interrelations between humanitarianism and the survival of our planet. Cash-based initiatives change the system itself in shifting from material to financial flows to beneficiaries. Finally, technological innovations may need to be changed and reconsidered before being applied to this system.

9.2   CHALLENGING SYSTEM BOUNDARIES: GREENING HUMANITARIAN SUPPLY CHAINS

While much of sustainable SCM research touches on various dimensions of sustainability, including social, environmental, economic, ethical, and health and safety considerations, it needs to be recognised that these dimensions are not of equal importance, after all. Anything that undermines Earth's survival may also put an end to humanity, even if the planetary level of analysis may seem remote from a supply chain perspective (Wieland, 2021). Humanitarianism is inherently anthropocentric, and yet, even from a humanitarian perspective, planetary health is of utmost importance for humanity's existence, putting the environment before society and the economy (de León et al., 2021).

Climate change alters the patterns of many hydro-meteorological hazards, whether talking of storms (and their larger versions such as hurricanes, cyclones, typhoons), various types of floods, heat and cold waves, or droughts. It changes their frequency, timing, location, and severity—not to speak of their cascades in terms of vector- and water-borne diseases, food insecurity, and/ or displacement and migration. Changes in hazard patterns result in changing humanitarian needs, and from a supply chain perspective, these changes translate into differences in demand quantities, locations, and timing—pretty much everything that forecasting is about. Climate change is also a factor to incorporate in humanitarian logistical decisions (Yan, 2023). At the same time, humanitarians are also called upon in the aftermath of ecocides, as in the case of the Khakovka dam explosion.

The humanitarian community has recently also recognised their own role with regards to climate change. This has translated into many parallel greening endeavours. Just as in sustainable SCM, there are those that focus on waste avoidance and greening procurement, others that focus on greening transportation, and yet others on waste management. Unique to the sector is that reverse logistics is largely absent—primarily since extended producer responsibility requirements rarely apply to humanitarian efforts. At the same time, however, the sector has recognised the interrelations between the adoption of bio-based plastics and food security on the one hand when it comes to starch-based plastics, and deforestation on the other in the case of cellulose-based plastics. Due to this recognition, many humanitarian organisations have come to the conclusion to avoid these types of bioplastics altogether. However, plastic waste remains one of the largest problems of the sector, whereby much of the focus lies on eliminating plastic wherever possible.

Last but not least, humanitarian efforts often take place in an environment that either has little or dilapidated infrastructure, or where the extant infrastructure has been damaged by a disaster or conflict. Greening efforts have therefore paid much attention to sustainable energy sources, with a prime focus on solar, and to some extent, wind power. But here, too, humanitarian organisations have been avoiding biofuels for the same reasons that they undermine food security or lead to deforestation.

9.3   CHALLENGING THE SYSTEM: CASH-BASED INITIATIVES

Cash-based initiatives (CBIs) arguably eliminate product and material flows in humanitarian aid altogether, changing the 'commodity' from materials to financial flows. CBIs constitute a complete rethinking of the system whereby humanitarian supply chains do not provide items and services but the means for beneficiaries for themselves to decide and purchase what they need. Quite akin social welfare in many countries, the idea is to support people in making their own decisions. Also, just like social welfare, some of the money can come with strings attached (called earmarking or conditional cash) what it can be used for, but the trend is towards removing such restrictions and offering 'multipurpose' cash instead. One of the most important reasons to use CBIs is to empower beneficiaries (Heaslip et al., 2018), restoring the purchasing power and the dignity of recipients, while humanitarian supply chains instead need to vet financial service providers (Harpring, 2023) or even to make sure that retailers are available where needed. Interesting approaches include the incentivisation of retailers to come to a refugee camp, for example, or for mobile vendors to periodically visit otherwise remote communities.

Providing the financial means to buy something rather than providing materials is not always possible, however. There are times in which certain materials are just not available in an area, or in which hyperinflation might instantly erode purchasing power. In many cases, some types of materials might be available but others are not, necessitating a combination of cash and material provisions through the humanitarian supply chain. Furthermore, programmes that have been set up as CBIs may fail when conditions change. For example, at the end of 2019, Zimbabwe ran out of food to buy, and cash for food programmes needed to be quickly converted into importing food to the country. It requires quite some logistical knowledge to spot what is possible under which circumstances, and when to switch from one delivery modality or mechanism to another. Learning from such instances, humanitarian organisations have started to endow cash officers with logistical functions.

While CBIs empower recipients, they remain disputed for other reasons. The main criticism is that recipients may use the money for other than the intended means. There is little evidence that would underpin such misuse. A newer criticism, however, stems from questioning what recipients would buy and whether their preferences would align with the greening initiatives of humanitarian organisations. This would call for a stronger focus on educating respondents in the first place.

9.4   CHALLENGING SYSTEM COMPONENTS: ADAPTING NEW TECHNOLOGIES TO THE HUMANITARIAN CONTEXT

There are plenty of new technologies entering the humanitarian context. Some of them are mere applications of the same technologies that are applied elsewhere, but there are also some unique ones. For example, drones that have been adopted in this context have brought change in health care delivery—for example in Rwanda, which was the first country to adopt a complex hub-and-spoke drone delivery system for medical deliveries across health care centres, overcoming both large distances to remote areas, as well as the mountainous terrain of the country. The use of drones comes with its own possibilities for eliminating contagion in medical deliveries to quarantine zones, for example, but also with its own challenges in war zones, where it is impossible for people to distinguish between a 'good' humanitarian drone versus one that brings destruction.

Additive manufacturing has also been used in the humanitarian context. Examples include prostheses measured for patients in conflict zones, or pipe connections in water and sanitation programmes in remote environments. What is more, it is the ultra-cold chain of the Ebola STRIVE vaccine that has been used as a benchmark for developing ultra-cold chains for Covid-19 vaccination programmes around the world. Hand-in-hand with the temperature control requirements of the ultra-cold chain, temperature-tracking devices have finally been implemented also across the humanitarian supply chain.

Much discussed is the use of social media for needs assessment. Technological development has taken large leaps in this area, with better triangulation nowadays being possible in needs assessment, and with more people having access to phones and thereby a diminishing—but not completely eradicated—digital divide. Importantly, however, the humanitarian imperative is to assist people in need, and it is not an option to overlook the most vulnerable people. Furthermore, the very disaster one responds to may have wiped out the telecommunications infrastructure of entire regions, and the most relevant data for needs assessment may be the sudden lack of data from a particular city or island.

Many technologies that have revolutionised other sectors are difficult to adopt in the humanitarian context, however. For example, electric vehicles can rarely face the dust of dirty roads, and the maintenance and repair operations of many digital technologies are challenging to arrange in the remote circumstances or the conflict environments of humanitarian operations. This has been a prime challenge for adopting green transportation. Overall, technology development for the humanitarian context calls for a stronger focus on robustness and longevity of products and technologies, or at least a workaround whereby they would be operational without their digital features. After all, when everything else fails, humanitarians need to be able to deliver.

9.5   CONCLUDING RECOMMENDATIONS

Humanitarian supply chains are not immune to systemic changes. This chapter highlights three of them: greening efforts, change in commodities, and technological change. Importantly, these changes are somewhat different from their implications in commercial supply chains. For example, there is a vital recognition of the interplay between bioplastics and biofuel versus food security, deforestation, and climate change.

Changes from material to financial flows lend themselves to restructuring the humanitarian supply chain altogether. They reopen new questions, however, including that of product and material choices by beneficiaries. More needs to be done to educate the recipients of CBIs or to restrict the use of CBIs to mitigate potential adverse effects. The same is true for the implementation of new technologies: a refocus on robustness is essential for them to be operational also in the humanitarian sector. However, the same robustness may also support other sectors at the same time, reducing energy needs and the energy footprint of the supply chain.

ACKNOWLEDGEMENT

This research is part of the WORM project which received funding from the European Union's Horizon Europe research and innovation programme under grant agreement No. 101135392.

REFERENCES

Altay, N., Heaslip, G., Kovács, G., Spens, K., Tatham, P., & Vaillancourt, A. (2023). Innovation in humanitarian supply chains: a systematic review. *Annals of Operations Research*, 1-23, https://doi.org/10.1007/s10479-023-05208-6

Altay, N., Kovács, G., & Spens, K. (2021). The evolution of humanitarian logistics as a discipline through a crystal ball. *Journal of Humanitarian Logistics and Supply Chain Management*, 11(4), 577-584.

de León, E.A., Shriwise, A., Tomson, G., Morton, S., Lemos, D.S., Menne, B., & Dooris, M. (2021). Beyond building back better: imagining a future for human and planetary health. *The Lancet Planetary Health*, 5(11), e827-e839.

Harpring, R. (2023). Preparing for cash and voucher assistance – developing capabilities and building capacities. In: Heaslip, G., & Tatham, P. (eds.), *Humanitarian Logistics*, 4th ed., 217-246, Kogan Page.

Heaslip, G., Kovács, G., & Haavisto, I. (2018). Cash-based response in relief: The impact for humanitarian logistics, *Journal of Humanitarian Logistics and Supply Chain Management*, 8(1), 87-106.

Kovács, G., & Falagara Sigala, I. (2021). Lessons learned from humanitarian logistics to manage supply chain disruptions. *Journal of Supply Chain Management*, 57(1), 41-49.

Maghsoudi, A., Harpring, R., Piotrowicz, W.D., & Heaslip, G. (2023). Cash and voucher assistance along humanitarian supply chains: a literature review and directions for future research. *Disasters*, 47(1), 42-77.

Seuring, S., Aman, S., Hettiarachchi, B.D., de Lima, F.A., Schilling, L., & Sudusinghe, J.I. (2022). Reflecting on theory development in sustainable supply chain management. *Cleaner Logistics and Supply Chain*, 3, 100016.

van Wynsberghe, A., & Comes, T. (2020). Drones in humanitarian contexts, robot ethics, and the human–robot interaction. *Ethics and Information Technology*, 22, 43-53.

Wieland, A. (2021). Dancing the supply chain: Toward transformative supply chain management. *Journal of Supply Chain Management*, 57(1), 58-73.

Yan, Q. (2023). The use of climate information in humanitarian relief efforts: A literature review. *Journal of Humanitarian Logistics and Supply Chain Management*, 13(3), 331-343.

10. Circular economy

Philip Beske-Janssen

10.1 INTRODUCTION

Our economic system is, at its core, a linear system based on the logic of 'take-make-use-dispose'. This system has led to unprecedented levels of economic growth and global interconnectedness. The linear economy relies on large amounts of cheap materials and energy, mostly taken from finite natural resources in the form of fossil fuels or raw materials extracted from the earth. At the same time, it produces a huge amount of waste, most of which ends up in landfills or incinerators, or worse, is simply dumped into the environment, polluting it. Obviously, such a linear system will eventually reach a point where most of the resources are consumed and the waste grows to unmanageable amounts (Korhonen et al., 2018). Against this background, the concept of a circular economy, 'take-make-use-reuse', has received increasing attention in recent years (Geissdoerfer et al., 2017). However, the transition to a circular economy represents a systemic shift that builds long-term resilience, creates business and economic opportunities, and delivers environmental and societal benefits (Webster, 2015).

Among the first to explore the concept of a circular economy (CE) were Stahel and Reday-Mulvey (1976), who focused on the industrial economy. They introduced the idea of a circular economy and outlined strategies for waste prevention, regional job creation, resource efficiency and dematerialisation of the industrial economy. Stahel (1982) also emphasised the importance of selling the use rather than ownership of goods, and presented a sustainable business model for the circular economy that allowed industry to profit without externalising the costs and risks associated with waste.

Over time, the understanding of CE and its practical application have evolved, incorporating various features and contributions from concepts that share the idea of closed loops. Influential theories include cradle-to-cradle (McDonough and Braungart, 2002), the laws of ecology (Commoner, 1971), the performance economy (Stahel, 2010), regenerative design (Lyle, 1996), industrial ecology (Isenmann, 2002), biomimicry (Benyus, 2002) and the blue economy (Pauli, 2010).

The most prominent definition for the CE comes from the Ellen MacArthur Foundation (2013), which describes CE as 'an industrial economy that is restorative or regenerative by intention and design' (p. 14). A rather comprehensive definition is provided by Kirchherr et al. (2017, p. 224f) who define CE as

> an economic system that is based on business models which replace the 'end-of-life' concept with reducing, alternatively reusing, recycling and recovering materials in production/distribution and consumption processes, thus operating at the micro level (products, companies, consumers), meso level (eco-industrial parks) and macro level (city, region, nation and beyond), with the aim to accomplish sustainable development, which implies creating environmental quality, economic prosperity and social equity, to the benefit of current and future generations.

However, while these can be seen as fairly comprehensive definitions, the understanding of CE is still very diverse, and there is a large number of definitions and different schools of thought. In short, the understanding of CE is still contested, especially when considering both academics and practitioners, generalists and experts, pioneers and opportunists. Nevertheless, there are several overlapping concepts that transcend these differences and can be observed in most of the different iterations of CE.

First, CE is often associated with eco-efficiency, which is a targeted approach to minimise the consumption of primary energy and virgin materials and reduce waste generation. This is achieved by increasing the efficiency of both production and consumption processes, thereby reducing the negative environmental impacts associated with industrial production (Ghisellini et al., 2016). The fundamental goal of eco-efficiency is to create value while reducing environmental impacts (Huppes and Ishikawa, 2005). This dual focus on economic and environmental benefits highlights the two main motivations for adopting a circular approach. This can be understood as a simplified perception of CE and is primarily associated with waste management strategies such as the 3Rs: reduce, reuse and recycle (Ghisellini et al., 2016).

However, such a reductionist view does not fully capture the comprehensive nature of CE, which goes beyond waste management to include a wider range of strategies aimed at creating a sustainable economic system. This is where the concept of eco-effectiveness comes in. Eco-effectiveness is a transformative approach that re-imagines products and their associated material flows in such a way that they form a supportive relationship with both ecological systems and economic growth (Borrello et al., 2020, p. 12). The aim of eco-efficiency is to create circular cycles that allow materials to retain their value as resources rather than being discarded as waste. This requires innovative approaches to material production, product design and the structuring of industrial systems and business models. The ultimate goal is to generate positive value in three dimensions: economic, environmental and social (Borrello et al., 2020).

In line with this, most CE concepts include the idea of a regenerative and even restorative design of the system. The aim is not only to limit current environmental degradation, but also to ensure the regeneration of natural ecosystems that have already been damaged or even destroyed. To achieve this goal, CE aims to remove waste from the very beginning of a product's design phase. In addition, the perception of waste is changed to waste as a resource. In industrial ecology, for example, the production facilities of different organisations are linked in such a way that the by-products of one company, commonly considered waste, can be used by another company in the network as a resource for its own production. One of the earliest and largest examples of what is commonly called an 'eco-industrial park' is the Kalundborg Symbiosis in Denmark (www.symbiosis.dk). Such a change of perspective should help to bring forward another common denominator of the different CE perspectives, namely the maximisation of resource use and value contribution (Bocken et al., 2016). This also includes a shift from the previously mentioned idea of product ownership to product use through leasing, renting or sharing (Swapfiets, 2022).

10.2   CIRCULAR ECONOMY IN A SUPPLY CHAIN MANAGEMENT CONTEXT

A functioning CE relies on networks of individual actors that align their strategies and processes to ensure maximum resource utilisation (Ritzén and Sandström, 2017). To make this possible, CE takes a systemic view, such as that of traditional supply chain management (SCM) theory. Furthermore, companies are faced with the challenge of integrating social and environmental issues into their supply chains (Busse et al., 2017) and rely to varying degrees on sustainable supply chain management (SSCM) (Seuring and Müller, 2008) or reverse logistics to meet this challenge. With CE, more options for integrating sustainability into supply chains are emerging, and companies are using strategies from SSCM to develop circular supply chains that at least aim to address environmental issues (Geissdoerfer et al., 2018). The interconnectedness of different entities in the system, the linear material and energy flows and their return and reuse to minimise waste are clear indications of this influence. However, the different research streams of CE, SSCM and reverse logistics are currently not well integrated (Hazen et al., 2021), and CE could benefit from the experience of reverse logistics, for example, for the development of take-back schemes. Nevertheless, relevant publications have already established this link. For example, Batista et al. (2018) have distinguished between closed loops, which keep materials within a supply network, and open loops, which span different supply chains in the sense that the materials or waste of one supply chain (actor) can become the resource of another supply chain, thus linking actors from different networks.

In addition, researchers have linked SCM and CE on a stronger conceptual basis by identifying key concepts. Bocken et al. (2016) introduced the concept of three principles for enabling circular energy and material flows. Specifically, they proposed the concepts of closing, slowing and narrowing these loops. In their work, Geissdoerfer et al. (2018) extended this by additionally focusing on specific activities within these loops. They proposed to include the concepts of intensifying loops and dematerialising loops. Each of these concepts represents a unique strategy for achieving a more sustainable and efficient use of resources, which will be briefly discussed below. Konietzko et al. (2020), while not using all five different concepts, extended the conceptual development by adding 'regenerate', which includes the use of renewable energy and non-toxic materials, and 'inform', which refers to the use of information technology to promote circularity.

1. Closing loops: This concept refers to the practice of reusing materials through recycling, remanufacturing and similar processes. The aim is to create a closed-loop system in which waste is minimised by turning it back into raw materials for new products. This not only reduces the need for virgin materials, but also reduces the amount of waste sent to landfill. Examples of closed loops include recycling plastic bottles into new ones, or remanufacturing used car parts into new components.

2. Slowing loops: This concept is about extending the life of products and materials. It involves the design of durable goods and the implementation of product life cycle extensions such as repair, maintenance and refurbishment. By slowing down the rate at which products are consumed and discarded, we can reduce the overall demand for new products and the resources needed to produce them. For example, a smartphone designed to be easily repairable can significantly extend its life, slowing the cycle of consumption and waste.

3. Intensifying loops: This concept diverts from the three principles suggested by Bocken et al. (2016). Geissdoerfer et al. (2018) introduced a more value-intensive use phase of materials or products with this concept. It promotes the idea of pooled or shared product use over individual consumption. This can be seen in the rise of the sharing economy, where products such as cars, bicycles or even houses are shared by multiple users. This intensifies the use of these products, maximising their value and reducing the need for each individual to own one.

4. Narrowing the loops: This concept is about overall resource efficiency, using fewer resources per product. It involves optimising production processes and improving product design to reduce the number of raw mate-

rials needed. This could include using lightweight materials in product design or implementing energy-efficient manufacturing processes. The aim is to close the resource loop by minimising the input of resources and reducing the output of waste. Such a strategy does not affect the speed of product and material flows, which distinguishes it from the first three concepts. In addition, it does not involve a service, such as repair, in the case of slowing down the loops.

5. Dematerialisation of loops: This concept refers to the substitution of products for services in a way that increases the utility and longevity of products and materials. This is often seen in the shift from product ownership to product-service systems, where consumers pay for the service a product provides rather than owning the product itself. For example, instead of buying a car (a product), a person might use a car-sharing service (a service), which can result in fewer cars being produced and a reduction in resource consumption.

10.3   THE BUTTERFLY DIAGRAM

The Ellen MacArthur Foundation's Circular Economy System Diagram, commonly referred to as the Butterfly Diagram (Figure 10.1), can be seen as one of the most influential frameworks for summarising circular economy concepts. It takes the five principles outlined above and transforms them into a visualisation of the interconnected systems that underpin them. The name Butterfly Diagram comes from the distinctive shape of the diagram. In the centre are the various process steps required to deliver a product or service, essentially representing the current linear economy. Outside these linear process steps are two interconnected loops on the right and left, representing the biological and technical cycles of resource flows. Both loops are inspired by the idea of continuously preserving and regenerating value through cycles of recovery and restoration (Ellen MacArthur Foundation, 2013). The diagram shows how resources, including waste as a resource, continuously flow in these loops through different iterations of process steps, thereby extracting maximum value from the different resources throughout their life cycle, while avoiding or at least minimising waste that cannot be reused and eventually ends up in landfill.

10.3.1   The Centre of the Butterfly Diagram

The centre between the two outer circles of the diagram, the butterfly body, represents a production system that at first glance resembles normal linear production. It links the initial extraction of materials and generation of energy with the final disposal of waste. In between, a simplified version of a supply

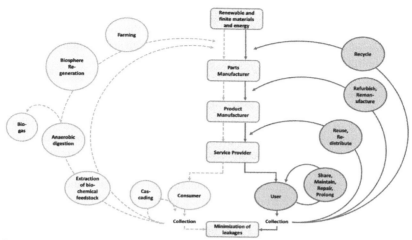

Source: Based on Ellen MacArthur Foundation, 2013.

Figure 10.1   The Butterfly Diagram

chain, consisting of parts manufacturers, product manufacturers and service providers, allows consumers, in the case of biological materials, or users, in the case of technological materials, to buy and use services or products. This distinction is a first indication that this is not a visualisation of normal linear production. It emphasises the idea that products of a biological nature are consumed and eventually returned to the natural environment, and that products or services based on technological materials are used, which includes the sharing of products or products as a service. This understanding allows for a perspective of customers not as ultimate owners, but rather as users of a product or service to meet a particular need at a particular time. In reality, of course, products may be made up of biological and technological materials which, at some point in their life cycle, would need to be separated in order to be managed in their respective cycles.

Another difference is the addition of a service provider step rather than a retailer step. This distinction is intended to emphasise the idea of services as a way of meeting customer needs. This can take the form of products as a service, leasing business models or other means of sharing or extending the life of products, thereby increasing their utilisation.

The addition of this seemingly very similar version of a linear supply chain also shows that circular supply chains will be based to a certain extend on linear production and service processes. While important, radical and disruptive changes are needed to make the transition to circular supply chains, much of the research, practical experience, practices and even infrastructure that have made linear supply chains so efficient should not be ignored. Reverse logistics, for example, is an integral part of closing the loops, as is the implementation of sustainability in supply chains to mitigate and minimise environmental pollution and social injustice.

10.3.2   The Biological Cycle of the Butterfly Diagram

The left side of the butterfly diagram represents the biological cycle, which includes consumer products made primarily from organic, bio-based or biodegradable materials. These materials are able to biodegrade and safely return to the earth. While the cycle mainly applies to consumer products such as food, it also includes other biodegradable materials such as cotton or wood. Over time, these materials can move from the technical cycle to the biological cycle once they have degraded beyond the point at which they can be used to make new products. Processes such as composting and anaerobic digestion facilitate this return, allowing the land to regenerate essential nutrients. These nutrients can then be used to make new biodegradable materials, contributing to the continuation of natural processes and the preservation of the environment.

10.3.2.1 Cascading of materials for maximum resource utilization

Cascading is an integral strategy in the biological cycle of the butterfly diagram. Through cascading, resource use and economic value from renewable resources can be maximised over multiple life cycles. When products or materials reach the end of their useful life and cannot be reused, they enter the outer loops of the biological cycle and return to the soil. This is based on keeping products in use for as long as possible and only using processes such as anaerobic digestion in biogas plants for energy recovery as a last resort.

An example would be a chair made of solid wood, a renewable biological resource. After its first use as a chair, possibly several generations or at least different owners, the chair may have reached the point where it can no longer be properly maintained. In this case, the wood can be recycled into a new form of material. For example, it can be ground up and reused to make chipboard. This could possibly be returned to the soil after its use phase, or the boards could be burned for energy and the ash returned to the soil as fertiliser for new plants. However, this last option would result in a 'loss' of material and is therefore, as mentioned above, only a last resort.

10.3.2.2 Renewable materials

Central to the CE is the concept of regeneration, which focuses on (re)building natural capital and avoiding further depletion of the earth's limited resources. BioPanel is a company that uses hemp to produce panels for a variety of applications, such as road signs, as a renewable and biodegradable alternative to the metal and oil-based plastics that are mainly used today (biopanel.nl). The material is based on hemp grown specifically for the production of the panels, which extracts CO_2 from the atmosphere and binds it for the lifetime of the product. At the end of their life, the products are fully biodegradable, returning nutrients to the soil or being recycled into a new bio-based resource.

Ideally, the CE revolves around consumables made from organic, bio-based or biodegradable materials that can be safely composted or digested. It emphasises the return of nutrients to the ecosystem and the optimisation of natural processes. Biopanel is an example of how this cycle can be effectively implemented, reducing waste and harnessing the value of hemp. Ultimately, the biological cycle plays a crucial role in the circular economy, promoting the regeneration of the earth and the development of sustainable alternatives.

10.3.3   The Technical Cycle of the Butterfly Diagram

The right-hand cycle of the butterfly diagram represents the technical cycle, which focuses on non-consumable goods made from durable, non-biodegradable and usually finite materials. This cycle aims to maintain and extend the life of these materials through processes called loops, such as reuse, repair, remanufacture or recycling. Each loop connects a production step further downstream from the central, linear process stream with a process step further upstream. Ideally, each product is kept in the innermost loops for as long as possible before entering a further outward layer. This is because the innermost loops require significantly less energy and additional resources to reuse the product, or in other words, the innermost loops have greater value retention because they keep a product intact for as long as possible (Reike et al., 2018). In other words, using a functioning product and keeping it intact for as long as possible is less energy and resource intensive than dismantling it, making the innermost loop, sharing, maintaining and reusing the preferred option over refurbishing or recycling. The different loops are introduced with an illustrative example. The loops are arranged in the order of their preferred use as outlined above.

10.3.3.1 Share, maintenance and repair

This innermost loop aims to maintain products at their highest level of utility. It is based on the idea of extending the life of a product in relatively unchanged form for as long as possible. In addition, the individual use of a product should be intensified as much as possible. The latter can be seen in the use of a car by an individual or a normal household. On average, the actual use, such as transporting passengers from one place to another, is around 8%, while the remaining 92% of the car's life is spent in parking (Ellen MacArthur

Foundation, 2019). Sharing services, such as drive now (www.drivenow.com), try to increase the utilisation rate by allowing a large number of potential users to access the cars, thereby reducing their idle time.

Maintenance and repair are concerned with prolonging the life of an individual product so that it can continue to meet the user's needs. Maintenance refers to simple actions such as cleaning and caring for a product. Repair can involve replacing parts or other processes such as sewing a textile product. An example is Patagonia's 'Worn Wear' programme, which encourages customers to repair their gear, thereby reducing the need for replacement (Patagonia, 2023).

Such strategies follow different concepts, as outlined above. Firstly, they should dematerialise the loops in the sense that users do not have to buy individual products. They also intensify use by giving access to more users through sharing. In addition, by limiting the production of new products, such strategies aim to close loops by reversing supply chain processes and returning them to their original users. In this sense, they also slow down loops, as repaired or maintained products can substitute for new products and reduce the speed of material flows.

10.3.3.2 Reuse, redistribution

The second most common loop encourages the reuse of products in their current form. The idea behind this strategy is also to prolong the life of a product in its unchanged form. It can be combined with the first loop to keep the product in working condition. If a user no longer wants to use the product, they can decide to keep it, throw it away or redistribute it to the potential user base by donating or selling it to a new user. This last case follows the redistribution concept. A classic example is a flea market where products are redistributed to new users. Today, to scale this up, companies such as eBay have introduced platforms to facilitate the process. Others have made it part of their business model, such as Freitag, which allows customers to swap their bags with other users. In this way, they can maintain the feeling of getting something 'new' for themselves, without the resources and energy needed to create this new product from scratch (Freitag, 2023). It also caters to users who are either unable or unwilling to pay the price for new products, but rely on secondary markets for their product needs. IKEA, for example, has launched a buy-back scheme where customers can sell back their old furniture for store credit (IKEA, 2023).

Overall, such a strategy follows a similar conceptual idea of closing, slowing down, intensifying and narrowing the loops. It also shows that the difference between, for example, sharing and redistributing products can be very fine and that companies need to be careful to address this in their respective business models.

10.3.3.3 Refurbishment, remanufacture

This loop involves returning products to like-new condition, perhaps even to a higher standard than before. It involves replacing defective parts with functional parts. These parts can be either new or taken from returned products. Typical examples are large copying and printing machines, often used in offices. During their lifetime, parts such as the sheet feeder may fail and can be replaced with a working one. Companies such as Kyocera are pursuing such a strategy. Ideally, such products are designed so that individual components can be easily dismantled, making refurbishment or remanufacturing quick and easy. Remanufacturing is generally understood as a more thorough process that involves dismantling the entire product and reassembling it to original specifications. Refurbishment, however, focuses on the parts that are actually damaged and is therefore a simpler solution, but does not always achieve the same quality. Refurbishing or remanufacturing is not limited to smaller products, but has long been used in the construction industry, for example, where houses are upgraded with new heating, windows or wiring. It can also be used as a business model on an industrial scale. Renault, for example, has a refurbishment plant for used cars, reducing environmental impact and offering customers low-cost cars (Renault, 2021).

Once again, the aim is to extend the life of a product, either by keeping it functional for longer or by upgrading it to meet customer needs as trends and technologies evolve. Again, the concepts of closing, narrowing, slowing down and redistributing are applied, although the investment in new materials and energy will be higher than in the previous two.

10.3.3.4 Recycling

This is the least desirable cycle, where materials are broken down and used to make new materials. Such a process ultimately destroys the original product and attempts to maximise the stored value of its constituents. Often this means 'downcycling' the quality of a material, as it is a challenge to recycle materials to their original specifications. For example, PET plastic bottles could be recycled into a blended fabric that can be used to make polyester sweaters. These sweaters, when recycled, can be made into a park bench, and at the end of their life the plastic could end up in the asphalt of a road. Eventually, the material would end up in a landfill. So, recycling often extends the life of a material, but ultimately it just delays the generation of unusable waste. An opportunity arises when materials are used that can be recycled almost indefinitely while retaining their original, primary, quality. One such material is aluminium. Approximately 75% of all aluminium ever produced is still in use today because of its recyclability. Novelis, the world's largest aluminium rolling and recycling company, is an example of an organisation that has embraced this strategy and meets almost 60% of its raw material needs with recycled content (Novelis, 2023).

There is already regulation for a recycled content quota for certain materials, such as plastics, and this will further increase the need for recycled materials. At the same time, some regulations, such as health and safety regulations for food packaging, can be an obstacle to introducing higher recycled content in certain product categories. Even as a last resort, this loop has often been understood as the main strategy in the circular economy. While it will undoubtedly continue to play an important role, society, businesses and governments will need to challenge themselves further to ensure that the CE does not become a downcycling economic system, but actually retains the value of the materials.

Such a concept also aims to close the loop, as it was one of the first concepts to aim to return resources to their respective supply chains. It also tries to slow down the loops in the sense of not extracting new materials. Potentially, it also tries to reuse materials for completely different purposes, for example, in line with Batista et al.'s (2018) conceptualisation of loops in supply chains. In any case, this is the strategy that predominantly follows a resource efficiency approach and thus mainly tries to reduce resource loops. Currently, this seems to be the main strategy adopted by companies.

By integrating these cycles and loops, the Butterfly Diagram encapsulates the regenerative nature of the circular economy. It promotes the idea of keeping products, components and materials at their highest utility and value, while minimising waste and reducing dependence on finite natural resources. As a result, this model becomes a driver of innovation, offering economic, environmental and societal benefits in a world of increasing resource constraints.

As you move through the various stages of the technical cycle, it is important to focus on product design that meets the unique requirements of each stage. This could mean designing items for sharing or reuse to be more durable and withstand intensive use, or creating products that are easy to repair, have modular components for replacement and remanufacture, or are made from materials that can be easily separated for recycling. It is also important to design for multiple loops, such as creating repairable products using recyclable materials. One example is Fairphone, which designs durable smartphones with replaceable parts for easy maintenance by the customer. The phone is modular and certain parts, such as the camera, can be upgraded to meet new customer needs. Finally, the company promotes safe recycling to recover precious metals and reuse components. To this end, they have introduced a take-back system that customers can use to return phones from other companies (Fairphone, 2022). The Butterfly Diagram highlights the importance of prioritising the inner loops for value retention and cost savings, and the importance of designing products that are aligned with specific cycle steps. It also shows that the innermost loops can satisfy more of the five different circular economy concepts. In principle, all concepts can be associated with the innermost loops, but as we move outwards, fewer concepts become viable options.

10.3.4 Critical Reflection

Ghisellini et al. (2016) noted that while the circular economy is gaining recognition as a more sustainable alternative to traditional economic models, it is clear that the actual implementation of circular strategies and activities is still in its infancy and may, to its fullest extent, be an unattainable utopia.

Firstly, there will never be a 100% CE or circular supply chain in the foreseeable future. If a truly circular supply chain were to be established, the laws of thermodynamics will always result in energy and also material losses, making it impossible to have a completely closed loop. As Cullen (2017, p. 483) puts it: 'Every loop around the circle creates dissipation and entropy, attributed to losses in *quantity* (physical material losses, by-products) and *quality* (mixing, downgrading). New materials and energy must be injected into any circular material loop, to overcome these dissipative losses.' However, this should not deter us from aiming for as much circularity as possible. Rather than not starting the transition at all, the goal of the most circular CE must therefore be to recover these losses through renewable energy and materials.

In addition to this critical point, there are other aspects that represent a challenge or a valid criticism of the current implementation of CE. There are several barriers that make the transition to CE difficult. This transition is not just about implementing a few isolated initiatives or pilot projects. It requires a massive, widespread change in the way we produce and consume goods. This means that changes need to take place across entire industries and sectors, and even at the level of individual consumer behaviour (Korhonen et al., 2018). Furthermore, given the interconnectedness of the global economy, this shift needs to occur on a global scale.

Given the supply constraints, price volatility, sometimes poor quality, contamination, legacy issues and other inherent uncertainties associated with secondary resources, it is unlikely that companies would choose to use waste as a resource in a circular economy, as opposed to the well-established value chains with primary resources (Corvellec et al., 2022), which often are even cheaper to procure. In addition, the lack of consumer interest in green offers is a widespread problem. The circular economy requires a radical reformulation of the role of the consumer – from consumer to user. As a result, the idea of replacing traditional ownership with dematerialised services may not always be attractive or feasible for consumers (Corvellec et al., 2022).

Much of this criticism is further related to the current vague description and definition of CE, as mentioned above. As a result, this leads to a wide variety of circular business models with different approaches and understandings of circularity (Geissdoerfer et al., 2018). Furthermore, despite progress in recent years, there is still a significant challenge in the means to accurately measure the circularity of a business model (Korhonen et al., 2018) and the associated sustainability impacts. As a result, it is difficult and almost impossible to assess and compare the circularity of different approaches.

Even more fundamental is the criticism of the sustainability impacts of a CE. The environmental benefits promised by the circular economy, such as reduced material consumption or increased product use, could inadvertently trigger the rebound effect or the Jevons paradox. This occurs when a reduction in material use in production leads to lower product prices, which in turn leads to higher sales and ultimately higher resource use. Similarly, the dematerialisation of products could give users access to products they would not normally use, potentially leading to an increased environmental footprint. For example, car sharing could lead to more car use and a higher environmental impact due to increased exhaust emissions as access to cars becomes more widespread. However, the public discussion about CE is heavily influenced by companies who see an opportunity to continue their business, albeit in a changed form, undisturbed by criticisms about environmental destruction and resource scarcity. They see an opportunity for a 'world without limits to growth' (Accenture, 2014) and therefore often do not perceive this paradox as a problem, but an opportunity.

Furthermore, it is unclear how the circular economy model enhances social equity in terms of inter- and intra-generational fairness, gender, racial and religious equality, financial parity and equal opportunities. These important ethical and moral aspects seem to be overlooked in the current model (Murray et al., 2017), as the social dimension is generally not included in definitions and descriptions of CE (Geissdoerfer et al., 2018). Even the Butterfly Diagram explained in this chapter focuses on resources and energy and does not address society in a similar way. CE is dominated by a technological and environmental language, which is evident in the distinction between eco-efficiency and eco-effectiveness. There is little discussion of social efficiency or effectiveness. However, the transition to a circular economy will inevitably create inequalities. Some sectors, regions and groups will benefit more than others, and some may even suffer. For example, workers in certain sectors may lose their jobs, while others in emerging green industries may gain. As more industries and nations rely on recycled materials, markets for virgin materials will suffer. That is why it is crucial to manage this transition in a way that promotes social justice and ensures a fair distribution of benefits and burdens. This transition requires proactive social policies and measures to support those who are negatively affected (Korhonen et al., 2018).

It is therefore a mistake to use the circular economy as a synonym for sustainable development, as is often done. Only by fully integrating sustainability can we create a sustainable economic system that harnesses the potential benefits of circularity (Geissdoerfer et al., 2018).

We must therefore be careful not to repeat the mistakes of the past, such as those made when trying to create sustainable supply chains. For a long time, the focus in this area was also mainly on environmental issues, while ignoring the social impacts along the supply chain (Beske and Seuring, 2014). The conversation has also been heavily influenced by companies that implement easy solutions to become more sustainable, essentially following eco-efficient rather than eco-effective solutions. These companies are often unwilling to make active changes towards more sustainable business practices, usually only responding to pressure from stakeholders. Eco-efficient approaches are also often dominant in companies' approaches to CE. Recycling and resource efficiency in production are the main strategies, rethinking product offerings and business models is less common.

In essence, the current CE discourse focuses on economic aspects, overlooks social dimensions and oversimplifies its environmental implications (Geissdoerfer et al., 2017). However, to move towards a truly circular economy, we need to think about the full life cycle of products and materials. A circular economy is not just about recycling or waste management. It is about rethinking the whole life of products and materials, from when they are made and used, to when and if they are thrown away. This means looking at the environmental and social impacts at each stage and finding ways to reduce them. However, this requires a level of thinking and analysis that is often lacking in current approaches to product design and materials management (Korhonen et al., 2018).

10.4 CONCLUSION

Moving from a 'take-make-use-dispose' system to a circular model requires a systemic shift that can deliver significant business and economic benefits while reducing environmental impacts. The circular economy, as visualised by the Ellen MacArthur Foundation's Butterfly Diagram, provides a comprehensive framework for rethinking the life cycle of products and materials. It promotes waste prevention, resource efficiency and the dematerialisation of the industrial economy, thereby promoting, at least, environmental sustainability. A constantly growing number of examples of companies implementing circular products, strategies and services are a testament to the potential of a circular economy.

However, the transition to a circular economy is not without challenges. It requires a level of systemic thinking and analysis that is often lacking in current approaches to product design and materials management. It also demands changes in our economic models, social norms, behaviours and regulatory frameworks to value and incentivize circularity.

The future of SCM lies in the successful integration of the circular principles. As we move forward, it is crucial to continue researching and innovating in this field, addressing the challenges, and capitalizing on the opportunities presented by the circular economy. This will contribute to the broader goals of sustainable development. The circular economy represents a paradigm shift in SCM, offering a path towards a more sustainable and resilient future. As we continue to explore and implement these principles, we are not just tweaking the existing system; we are fundamentally changing it, potentially paving the way for a more sustainable and equitable world.

Often the discussion on the implementation of sustainability strategies revolves around the inherent trade-offs that companies face (Seuring and Müller, 2008), but as Ünal and Sinha (2023) argued, while these trade-offs exist in a sustainable CE scenario, they can ultimately be overcome. They could even support the implementation of a fully circular strategy for sustainability, rather than just an eco-efficiency oriented one, as overcoming these trade-offs leads to finding comprehensive solutions (Ünal and Sinha, 2023). This is particularly important as more and more companies are stepping up their CE activities, and it is necessary to distinguish between those who are merely following a mitigation, minimisation (i.e., eco-efficiency) path and those who are truly investing in transforming business and society towards a more radical shift in mindset and practice to a regenerative economy.

Moving to a circular economy requires a big change. It is not just about making small changes to the existing system, it is about completely rethinking and changing it. It involves changing our economic models to create value, share value, repair, reuse, recycle or even not consume. It means changing our social norms and behaviours to support sustainable, circular patterns of consumption and production. Making such a big change is perhaps the most difficult challenge of all, as it requires us to break old habits, interests and power structures (Korhonen et al., 2018). We are at a crucial point in human existence. Implementing a circular economy can provide solutions to many of the challenges we face, and is therefore generally seen as a necessary path to take.

REFERENCES

Accenture (2014). Circular advantage: innovative business models and technologies to create value without limits to growth. https:// www .accenture .com/ t20150523t053139 __w __/ us -en/ _acnmedia/ accenture/ conversion -assets/ dotcom/ documents/global/pdf/strategy_6/accenture-circular-advantage-innovative-business -models-technologies-value-growth.pdf

Barreiro-Gen, M., & Lozano, R. (2020). How circular is the circular economy? Analysing the implementation of circular economy in organisations. *Business Strategy and the Environment*, 29(8), 3484-3494.

Batista, L., Bourlakis, M., Smart, P., & Maull, R. (2018). In search of a circular supply chain archetype–a content-analysis-based literature review. *Production Planning & Control*, 29(6), 438-451.

Benyus, J.M. (2002). *Biomimicry: Innovation inspired by nature*. Harper Collins.

Beske, P., & Seuring, S. (2014). Putting sustainability into supply chain management. *Supply Chain Management: An International Journal*, 19(3), 322-331.

Biopanel (2023). Eco-friendly and circular sheet material made of hemp and PLA. https://biopanel.nl/en/over-biopanel-2/

Bocken, N.M., De Pauw, I., Bakker, C., & Van Der Grinten, B. (2016). Product design and business model strategies for a circular economy. *Journal of Industrial and Production Engineering*, 33(5), 308-320.

Borrello, M., Pascucci, S., & Cembalo, L. (2020). Three propositions to unify circular economy research: A review. *Sustainability*, 12(10), 4069.

Busse, C., Schleper, M.C., Weilenmann, J., & Wagner, S.M. (2017). Extending the supply chain visibility boundary: Utilizing stakeholders for identifying supply chain sustainability risks. *International Journal of Physical Distribution & Logistics Management*, 47(1), 18-40.

Commoner, B. (1971). *The Closing Circle: Nature, Man, and Technology*. Random House Inc.

Corvellec, H., Stowell, A.F., & Johansson, N. (2022). Critiques of the circular economy. *Journal of Industrial Ecology*, 26(2), 421-432.

Cullen, J.M. (2017). Circular economy: Theoretical benchmark or perpetual motion machine? *Journal of Industrial Ecology*, 21(3), 483-486.

Ellen MacArthur Foundation (2013). Towards the circular economy vol. 1: An economic and business rationale for an accelerated transition. https:// www .elle nmacarthurfoundation .org/ towards-the-circular-economy-vol-1-an-economic-and -business-rationale-for-an

Ellen MacArthur Foundation (2019). Circular economy in cities – Urban mobility system. https:// elle nmacarthur foundation .org/ circular -economy -opportunity -and -benefit-factsheets

Fairphone (2022). Fairphone's Impact Report 2022 – Change is in your hands. https:// www.fairphone.com/wp-content/uploads/2023/05/Fairphone-Impact-Report-2022 .pdf

Freitag (2023). Shopping Without Any Payment. https://www.freitag.ch/en/swap

Geissdoerfer, M., Savaget, P., Bocken, N.M., & Hultink, E.J. (2017). The Circular Economy–A new sustainability paradigm? *Journal of Cleaner Production*, 143, 757-768.

Geissdoerfer, M., Morioka, S.N., de Carvalho, M.M., & Evans, S. (2018). Business models and supply chains for the circular economy. *Journal of Cleaner Production*, 190, 712-721.

Ghisellini, P., Cialani, C., & Ulgiati, S. (2016). A review on circular economy: the expected transition to a balanced interplay of environmental and economic systems. *Journal of Cleaner Production*, 114, 11-32.

Hazen, B.T., Russo, I., Confente, I., & Pellathy, D. (2021). Supply chain management for circular economy: Conceptual framework and research agenda. *The International Journal of Logistics Management*, 32(2), 510-537.

Huppes, G., & Ishikawa, M. (2005). Eco-efficiency and Its Terminology. *Journal of Industrial Ecology*, 9(4), 43-46.

IKEA (2023). Buyback & Resell. https://www.ikea.com/en/customer-service/services/buyback-pubfeb6cc00

Isenmann, R. (2002). Further efforts to clarify industrial ecology's hidden philosophy of nature. *Journal of Industrial Ecology*, 6(3-4), 27-48.

Kirchherr, J., Reike, D., & Hekkert, M. (2017). Conceptualizing the circular economy: An analysis of 114 definitions. *Resources, Conservation and Recycling*, 127, 221-232.

Konietzko, J., Bocken, N., & Hultink, E.J. (2020). Circular ecosystem innovation: An initial set of principles. *Journal of Cleaner Production*, 253, 119942.

Korhonen, J., Nuur, C., Feldmann, A., & Birkie, S.E. (2018). Circular economy as an essentially contested concept. *Journal of Cleaner Production*, 175, 544-552.

Lyle, J.T. (1996). *Regenerative design for sustainable development*. John Wiley & Sons.

McDonough, W., & Braungart, M. (2002). Design for the triple top line: new tools for sustainable commerce. *Corporate Environmental Strategy*, 9(3), 251-258.

Murray, A., Skene, K., & Haynes, K. (2017). The circular economy: an interdisciplinary exploration of the concept and application in a global context. *Journal of Business Ethics*, 140, 369-380.

Novelis (2023). 2022 Global sustainability report – shaping a sustainable world together. https://www.novelis.com/wp-content/uploads/2022/12/Novelis-FY2022-Sustainability-Report.pdf

Patagonia (2023). 'Worn wear stories'. https://eu.patagonia.com/dk/en/stories/worn-wear/

Pauli, G.A. (2010). *The Blue Economy: 10 Years, 100 Innovations, 100 Million Jobs*. Paradigm Publications.

Reike, D., Vermeulen, W.J., & Witjes, S. (2018). The circular economy: new or refurbished as CE 3.0?—Exploring controversies in the conceptualization of the circular economy through a focus on history and resource value retention options. *Resources, Conservation and Recycling*, 135, 246-264.

Renault (2021). Renault Group: 1st anniversary of the Refactory and inauguration of the Factory VO in Flins. https://media.renaultgroup.com/renault-group-1st-anniversary-of-the-refactory-and-inauguration-of-the-factory-vo-in-flins/

Ritzén, S., & Sandström, G.Ö. (2017). Barriers to the Circular Economy–integration of perspectives and domains. *Procedia Cirp*, 64, 7-12.

Schöggl, J.P., Stumpf, L., & Baumgartner, R.J. (2020). The narrative of sustainability and circular economy-A longitudinal review of two decades of research. *Resources, Conservation and Recycling*, 163, 105073.

Seuring, S., & Müller, M. (2008). From a literature review to a conceptual framework for sustainable supply chain management. *Journal of Cleaner Production*, 16(15), 1699-1710.

Stahel, W.R. (1982). The product life factor. An Inquiry into the Nature of Sustainable Societies: The Role of the Private Sector, Houston Area Research Center.

Stahel, W.R. (2010). *The performance economy* (2nd ed.). Palgrave Macmillan.

Stahel, W.R., & Reday-Mulvey, G. (1976). The potential for substituting manpower for energy: A report to the European Commission. Subsequently published as Jobs for tomorrow. New York: Vantage Press (1981).

Swapfiets (2022). Swapfiets Sustainability Report 2021. https://news.swapfiets.com/en-NL/214916-swapfiets-sustainability-report-2021

Ünal, E., & Sinha, V.K. (2023). Sustainability trade-offs in the circular economy: A maturity-based framework. *Business Strategy and the Environment*, 32, 4662-4682.

Webster, K. (2015). *The Circular Economy: A Wealth of Flows*. Ellen MacArthur Foundation Publishing.

Index

Printed and bound by CPI Group (UK) Ltd, Croydon, CR0 4YY

10/04/2025

14656068-0002